The Best of Casual American Cooking

DINER

SUNSET BOOKS
President and Publisher: Susan J. Maruyama
Director, Finance and Business Affairs: Gary Loebner
Director, Manufacturing and Sales Service: Lorinda Reichert
Director, Sales and Marketing: Richard A. Smeby
Editorial Director: Kenneth Winchester
Executive Editor: Robert A. Doyle

SUNSET PUBLISHING CORPORATION
Chairman: Jim Nelson
President/Chief Executive Officer: Robin Wolaner
Chief Financial Officer: James E. Mitchell
Publisher: Stephen J. Seabolt
Circulation Director: Robert I. Gursha
Editor, *Sunset Magazine:* William R. Marken

Produced by
WELDON OWEN INC.
President: John Owen
Publisher and Vice President: Wendely Harvey
Managing Editor: Lisa Chaney Atwood
Consulting Editor and Introductory Text: Norman Kolpas
Copy Editor: Sharon Silva
Design: Patty Hill
Production Director: Stephanie Sherman
Production Editor: Janique Gascoigne
Co-Editions Director: Derek Barton
Co-Editions Production Manager (US): Tarji Mickelson
Food Photographers: Allan Rosenberg, Allen V. Lott
Food Stylist: Heidi Gintner
Prop Stylist: Sandra Griswold
Assistant Food Stylists: Nette Scott, William Shaw
Assistant Prop and Food Stylist: Elizabeth Ruegg
Cover Photography: Joyce Oudkerk Pool
Cover Food Stylist: Susan Massey
Cover Prop Stylist: Carol Hacker
Half-Title Illustration: Martha Anne Booth
Glossary Illustrations: Alice Harth

Production by Kyodo Printing Co.
(S'pore) Pte Ltd
Printed in Singapore

First Printing 1995
10 9 8 7 6 5 4 3 2 1

ISBN 0-376-02037-7
Library of Congress Catalog Number: 95-067090

A Note on Weights and Measures:
All recipes include customary U.S. and metric measurements.
Metric conversions are based on a standard developed for these
books and have been rounded off. Actual weights may vary.

The Best of Casual American Cooking

DINER

by Diane Rossen Worthington

Contents

Introduction 7

Breakfast 17

Soup and Sandwiches 35

Blue Plate Specials 53

Side Dishes 79

Desserts 99

Introduction

*I*t's late night in the city, and you're dying for pie and coffee. Or you've left for work early and want to stop for breakfast. Maybe the family is doing weekend shopping, and the kids are hungry. Or you have tickets for a play, but there's only an hour to eat before showtime.

In America, only one kind of restaurant meets all these needs: the diner. With a menu ranging from luscious desserts to bountiful breakfasts, from three-course dinners to soups and sandwiches, it's the one place certain to please everyone. Here, office workers satisfy hunger on a budget. Teenagers gather after school for fries and sodas. Nightclubbers find quiet following an evening on the dance floor. Parents know that, even if the children are bouncing off the walls, they'll be welcomed—and will likely settle down over milk shakes and grilled cheese.

In short, the diner's appeal lies in the fact that it's about as close as you can come to feeling at home while eating out. Nowadays, folks yearn more than ever for the wholesome, generous food of this American institution and for its comfortable and welcoming atmosphere. With that yearning in mind, this book aims to help you re-create the diner experience in your own home.

Diner History

*D*iners began humbly in 1872, when Walter Scott, a pressman in Providence, Rhode Island, had the brainstorm of hitching a horse to a freight wagon, from which he served homemade sandwiches, pie and plates of sliced chicken to night-shift newspaper workers who had nowhere else to get a meal. The idea of these so-called lunch wagons quickly spread, with more elaborate operations providing a few indoor stools on which customers could perch while they ate. From there, it was a small step for the owners of these compact restaurants to unhitch their steeds, lower the wagons onto small pieces of inexpensive real estate, hook up to public utilities and stay open for business twenty-four hours a day.

Serving more than middle-of-the-night lunches, and drawing on an ever more diverse clientele, these round-the-clock establishments began to mimic the size, facilities and grandeur of the railroad's Pullman diners. By the early 1920s, the term diner had made its way into the vocabulary to describe this new breed of restaurants—already an American institution—that resembled permanently parked railway cars and offered breakfast, lunch and dinner, served anytime.

Diners thrived through the Great Depression. After all, people still had to eat, and diners offered generous, comforting food at bargain prices. But their heyday, perhaps, was reached amid the prosperity, growth and optimism of the 1950s. They were the restaurant of the common people, and every new suburb and old downtown district had to have one of its own.

In the face of competition from fast-food franchises, burgeoning suburban malls and civic redevelopment, diners continue to thrive today. New ones spring up regularly, offering burgers and fries, pancakes and meat loaf, bowls of soup and slices of pie in settings that pay tribute to classic diner architecture—particularly the sleek glass and chrome of the Streamline Moderne style or the Space Age–inspired Formica and Naugahyde of the fifties.

And Americans of every background and income continue to flock to them, knowing they'll be comfortable, cared for and well fed.

The Diner Experience

Some diners resemble the club car on a transcontinental train, with wood paneling, cozy leather booths and white-jacketed waiters. Others display the easy-to-clean surfaces of a busy city lunchroom—plastic laminate, glass and chrome. A country shack specializing in barbecue, with rickety walls and scarred tables, counts as a diner, too. So does a seaside shed where waitresses pile steamed crabs on tabletops lined with butcher paper.

What defines a diner is not so much these physical manifestations as the casual quality of the food and the warmth of the welcome. You might be greeted by a gum-snapping young waitress, a warm motherly figure or a gawky teen in a bow tie protruding from a too-big collar. No matter who it is, your server will instantly offer coffee or a fountain drink while you peruse the menu. (If they don't, start patronizing another diner!)

Once you've decided on what to eat, your order will be handed or called back to the cook, usually visible over the service counter in a kitchen only a little larger than a closet. If you're lucky, you might hear classic diner-speak—the colorful verbal shorthand waiters and waitresses have developed to communicate with the cooks. "Adam and Eve on a raft" signifies two poached eggs on toast. "Hold the grass" describes a sandwich without the lettuce garnish. A "cowboy with spurs" is a Western omelet served with french fries. And what could "cremate it" possibly mean? Toast the bread, of course.

A Diner at Home

The recipes on the pages that follow make it possible for you to cook and serve authentic diner food in your

own home, from waffles and pancakes to corned beef hash, from club sandwiches and chili to pot roast, from buttermilk biscuits to banana splits. Hearty, wholesome and definitive, they are ideal fare for family meals and casual dinner parties alike.

For an even more authentic touch, try setting a diner-style table to go with the meal.

Start with heavy institutional white china, either unadorned or decorated with a simple stripe around the rim. Or you might want to seek out diner tableware in one of the classic regional styles, such as California's signature Fiestaware or Western cowboy-style dishes adorned with cattle brands and lariats, that are returning to stores in reasonably priced reproductions.

Add a starched white or red-and-white checkered tablecloth, or, for that matter, an uncovered well-worn wooden or fifties' Formica tabletop; sturdy stainless-steel flatware; and chunky coffee mugs and tall fountain-style glasses to hold your choice of beverages (see following page). You'll have set the stage for a classic American dining experience.

Beverages

Late-night lunch wagons, precursors to the diners we know today, provided their patrons with few choices other than hot coffee. As diners spread and increased in size, their beverage offerings generally remained as simple as their selection of foods, most presenting only a single menu line listing coffee, tea and milk.

But, as diners spread nationwide, they came to embrace the favorite beverages of each national region. And the evolution of American tastes in refreshment was also reflected in the drinks that diners came to offer.

Fountain Drinks

In 1886, Atlanta pharmacist John Smyth Pemberton developed a sweet soda fountain drink made by combining carbonated water with a syrup flavored with extracts of coca leaf and kola nut. Trademarked in 1893 as Coca-Cola, the drink, along with Pepsi-Cola developed a few years later, became a nationwide favorite after World War I. No diner today would fail to serve cola, along with a selection of other carbonated beverages such as root beer, orange soda and any one of several lemon-lime drinks.

Soda pops or soft drinks, as they are often generically called, are also the foundation of other delightful soda-fountain creations. Add a scoop of vanilla ice cream to cola or root beer and you have an ice cream float. Process ice cream and soda together in a blender and you have a freeze or slush. Mix plain soda water with chocolate syrup and cold milk and you have the classic New York City egg cream, so named for the billowing meringuelike froth that forms on its surface. Combine soda water with sweetened lime juice and you get a lime rickey.

Drop the soda and replace it with milk and you enter a whole new realm of fountain drinks: milk shakes. With the range of ice creams and syrups, not to mention the addition of malt powder to make a malted (see sidebar, right), milk shakes become their own subculture of diner drinks.

Coffee, Tea and Chocolate

Coffee remains a diner standby, and a waitress or waiter is more than likely to offer you some the moment you take your seat. Diner coffee is typically brewed from a blend of medium-roasted beans: nothing spectacular to raise the eyebrows of today's coffee aficionado, but nonetheless full flavored and undeniably drinkable. What's more, the typical diner serves so much coffee that you'll seldom experience a bitter-tasting cup that has suffered from sitting on the hotplate too long.

Diner tea is usually orange pekoe bags brewed in the cup or a small pot. Such tea, in fact, can often yield a better-tasting beverage when brewed extra strong and poured over ice.

None of this is to say that you need to strive for authenticity when making coffee or tea to serve with diner food at home. Just as a handful

of enterprising establishments do today, try brewing your own favorite fresh-roasted beans or select teas to serve with breakfast or after lunch or dinner. And, for the children, by all means make their favorite hot chocolate to accompany their diner-style breakfasts or desserts.

Juices

Freshly squeezed orange juice and grapefruit juice are diner breakfast standbys. Seek out good juice oranges in your local market, or take a shortcut and buy the freshly squeezed juices on display in the produce departments or refrigerated cases of many food stores. Such canned juices as apple, cranberry and prune are also diner mainstays.

Plus, many people like to accompany their eggs with tomato juice or mixed-vegetable juice cocktail.

And don't forget one more diner favorite based on juice: lemonade, made by sweetening lemon juice with sugar, diluting it with water and serving it in ice-filled glasses.

Beer and Wine

Because they are family-oriented establishments, diners do not ordinarily serve alcoholic beverages. But a number of upscale diners today are breaking with tradition by offering a selection of beers and wines on their menus.

Diner fare doesn't call for breaking out the bottle of wine that's been aging in your cellar. Rather, your beverage should match the food's hearty, uncomplicated nature. For example, try an iced lager or ale from a local microbrewery with any sandwich in this book or with a robust blue plate special such as meat loaf or fried chicken. Spaghetti with meatballs or savory pot roast would be nicely complemented by a full-bodied red wine, while a big white would stand up well to roast turkey or stuffed pork chops. Let your choice of beverage reflect whatever festive tone you wish to set with your diner menu.

CHOCOLATE MALTED

Delight family and guests with this authentic soda-fountain treat. All you need is a blender and an appreciative audience standing by, because you must serve this frothy drink immediately. For the perfect slushy-thick texture, be sure not to overmix, and use extra-cold milk.

5   scoops vanilla ice cream
1¾   cups (14 fl oz/440 ml) cold milk
½   cup (4 fl oz/125 ml) chocolate syrup
3½   tablespoons malted milk powder

❖ In a blender, combine the ice cream, milk, chocolate syrup and malted milk powder. Blend until just mixed, with few or no lumps remaining. Serve at once in tall glasses, with a long teaspoon or a straw in each glass.

Serves 2

Basic Recipes

To make authentic diner meals at home, there are a few basic recipes you will need to master. Potatoes cooked every way—from creamy mashed spuds and crisp fries to onion-studded potatoes O'Brien—are popular side dishes. And, before you can make meat loaf, spaghetti or summer fruit pies, you'll need to have the basic recipes that follow.

MASHED POTATOES

Any kind of potato can be mashed. Waxy white, red or yellow varieties yield creamy purées, while baking potatoes produce the fluffier results usually found in diners. Evaporating the moisture after cooking the potatoes helps make them even lighter and fluffier when mashed.

3   lb (1.5 kg) white, red, yellow-fleshed or baking potatoes, peeled and cut into 2-inch (5-cm) pieces
1½ teaspoons salt, plus salt to taste
⅓   cup (3 oz/90 g) unsalted butter, cut into small pieces
1   cup (8 fl oz/250 ml) plus 2 tablespoons half-and-half (half cream), heated
    Ground white pepper

❖ In a large bowl, combine the potato pieces with water to cover and let stand for 5 minutes to remove excess starch. Drain.

❖ Bring a large saucepan three-fourths full of water to a boil. Add the 1½ teaspoons salt and the potatoes and return to a boil. Boil until tender when pierced with a fork, about 15 minutes. Drain well and return to the empty pan.

❖ Place the pan over high heat and, turning the potatoes to prevent scorching, heat to evaporate the moisture, 1–2 minutes. Remove from the heat. Using a potato masher, mash the potatoes until they are almost smooth. Add the butter, mash together, and then add the half-and-half, a little at a time, switching to a spoon when the potatoes are smooth. The potatoes should be creamy but not soupy.

❖ Season to taste with salt and white pepper, transfer to a warmed serving dish and serve immediately.

Serves 6

FRENCH FRIES

The secrets to success with french fries are drying the potatoes well before frying, keeping the oil at a constant temperature and not crowding the pan or covering it. If you plan to make these without an electric deep fryer, be sure you have a large, heavy-bottomed pan, a flat wire skimmer and a deep-fat frying thermometer. For "country-style" french fries, scrub the potatoes well but leave their skins on.

3   lb (1.5 kg) baking potatoes, each about 4 inches (10 cm) long
    Vegetable oil for deep-frying
    Salt

❖ Peel the potatoes, if desired, and cut them lengthwise into slices ⅜ inch (1 cm) wide. Then cut each slice lengthwise into strips ⅜ inch (1 cm) wide. Place in a large bowl, add water to cover and let stand for 5 minutes to remove excess starch.

❖ Pour oil to a depth of 2 inches (5 cm) in a deep-fat fryer or heavy saucepan and heat to 330°F (170°C), checking the temperature on the built-in thermometer or with a hand-held deep-fat frying thermometer.

❖ Line trays with paper towels.

❖ Drain the potatoes and pat dry with a clean kitchen towel. If using a deep-fat fryer, immerse the basket briefly in the oil to prevent the potatoes from sticking to it. Place 2 handfuls of the potatoes into the basket or onto a wire skimmer and lower it into the oil. (The oil will expand to cover the potatoes.) Fry until the potatoes are pale yellow but have not yet started to brown, 4–5 minutes. Raise the basket or remove the potatoes with the skimmer, drain for a moment over the pan, and transfer to paper towel–lined trays to drain for 10 minutes or for up to 2 hours. Repeat with the remaining potatoes, always returning the oil to the correct temperature before frying the next batch.

❖ Just before serving the fries, line additional trays with paper towels and reheat the oil to a temperature of 370°F (188°C). Fry the potatoes again, in batches, until golden brown and crisp, 3–5 minutes. Drain the basket or skimmer for a moment, then turn out the potatoes onto the towel-lined trays.

❖ Place the french fries in a serving bowl or basket, season to taste with salt and serve immediately.

Serves 6

POTATOES O'BRIEN

This recipe for crisp, panfried potatoes with peppers and onions originated in the early 1900s at a Manhattan restaurant known as Jack's. You can vary the recipe by substituting any of your favorite pepper varieties. Serve the potatoes with scrambled eggs, burgers or short ribs.

1½ tablespoons unsalted butter
1½ tablespoons olive oil
1   large yellow onion, finely chopped
½   small red bell pepper (capsicum), seeded, deribbed and finely diced
½   small green bell pepper (capsicum), seeded, deribbed and finely diced
2   lb (1 kg) small white or red potatoes, peeled and cut into ½-inch (12-mm) cubes
     Salt and freshly ground pepper
2   tablespoons finely chopped fresh parsley

❖ In a large frying pan over medium-high heat, melt ½ tablespoon of the butter with ½ tablespoon of the olive oil. Add the onion and sauté, stirring occasionally, until golden brown and just beginning to caramelize, 5–7 minutes. Do not allow the onion to scorch. Add the red and green peppers and sauté until beginning to soften, 3–5 minutes longer. Transfer to a serving bowl and set aside.

❖ Add ½ tablespoon each of the remaining butter and olive oil to the same pan. Add half of the cubed potatoes and cook, turning to brown all sides, 5–7 minutes. If the potatoes are too dry, add a little more butter or oil. Transfer the browned potatoes to the bowl holding the pepper mixture. Repeat with the remaining butter, olive oil and potatoes.

❖ Return the mixture to the pan. Raise the heat to high so that it quickly warms through. Remove from the heat and season to taste with salt and pepper. Add the parsley and stir to combine. Return to the serving bowl and serve immediately.

Serves 6

TOMATO SAUCE

We owe the all-American tomato sauce to Italian immigrants of the late 19th and early 20th century. Try it as a base for spaghetti sauce, or serve with eggs or meat loaf. For convenience, spoon the sauce into small containers or lock-top plastic bags and store in your freezer.

3   tablespoons olive oil
1   yellow onion, finely chopped
1   carrot, peeled and finely chopped
1   celery stalk, finely chopped
2   large cloves garlic, minced
2   cans (28 oz/875 g each) diced tomatoes, drained
1   can (28 oz/875 g) crushed tomatoes
3   tablespoons finely chopped fresh parsley
½   bay leaf
1   teaspoon dried oregano, crumbled
2   teaspoons dried basil, crumbled
1½ cups (12 fl oz/375 ml) water
1   teaspoon salt
¼   teaspoon freshly ground pepper

❖ In a large, heavy saucepan over medium heat, warm the olive oil. Add the onion, carrot and celery and sauté, stirring occasionally, until the vegetables are softened but not browned, 6–8 minutes. Add the garlic and sauté for 1 minute longer.

❖ Add the diced and crushed tomatoes, parsley, bay leaf, oregano, basil and water to the pan, cover partially and reduce the heat to medium-low. Simmer gently, stirring occasionally, until it has a well-rounded flavor, about 1 hour. Discard the bay leaf.

❖ In a food processor fitted with the metal blade or with a hand blender, purée the mixture until smooth. Return to the pan, if using a food processor. Stir in the salt and pepper. Continue to simmer the sauce briefly over medium-low heat to reduce it to the desired consistency, then taste and adjust the seasoning.

❖ Use immediately, or let cool, cover and refrigerate for up to 5 days or freeze for up to 2 months.

Makes about 2½ qt (2.5 l)

PIE CRUST

A good, flaky pie crust is a diner essential. This pastry can be made either in a food processor or by hand. It is then rolled out and baked in a pie plate to a light golden brown. The pie crust can be used for any one of a variety of pies, such as lemon meringue pie (recipe on page 107) or coconut custard pie (page 108).

1½ cups (7½ oz/235 g) all-purpose (plain) flour, plus flour for rolling dough
    Pinch of salt
2   tablespoons confectioners' (icing) sugar
½   cup (4 oz/125 g) unsalted butter, chilled, cut into small pieces
1   tablespoon vegetable shortening, chilled
1   egg yolk
¼   cup (2 fl oz/60 ml) ice water

14

❖ *To make the crust in a food processor fitted with the metal blade,* combine the 1½ cups (7½ oz/235 g) flour, the salt and confectioners' sugar. Process briefly to blend. Add the butter and shortening and process until the mixture resembles coarse meal, 5–10 seconds. With the motor running, add the egg yolk and ice water and process just until the dough begins to come together and holds a shape when pressed.

❖ *To make the crust by hand,* in a large bowl, combine the flour, salt and confectioners' sugar. Using a pastry blender, 2 knives or your fingertips, cut or rub in the butter and shortening until the mixture resembles coarse meal. Using a fork, gradually mix in the egg yolk and water just until the dough begins to come together and holds a shape when pressed.

❖ Transfer the dough made by either method to a lightly floured surface. Mold into a disk about ½ inch (12 mm) thick, wrap in plastic wrap and refrigerate for 1–2 hours or as long as overnight.

❖ Place the pastry disk on a lightly floured work surface and lightly dust the top with flour. Using a lightly floured rolling pin, roll out the dough into a round 11 inches (28 cm) in diameter, adding more flour if needed to prevent sticking.

❖ Gently ease the round into a 9-inch (23-cm) pie plate and press into the plate. Trim the edges, leaving a ½-inch (12-mm) overhang. Fold the overhang under, then crimp the edges attractively. Cover with plastic wrap and refrigerate for 2 hours.

❖ Preheat an oven to 350°F (180°C). Prick the bottom and sides of the pastry with a fork. Line the pastry with waxed paper and fill with pie weights or dried beans. Bake until the crust looks dry, about 20 minutes. Remove the weights or beans and the paper, return the crust to the oven and bake until golden brown, 5–10 minutes longer. Transfer to a rack and let cool completely.

Makes one 9-inch (23-cm) prebaked pie crust

Breakfast

*D*iner morning fare helps secure America's reputation for serving some of the best breakfasts in the world. Steaming hot coffee, continually replenished. Freshly squeezed orange juice, its color neon-bright. Plates heaped with eggs any way you like them, hash-browned potatoes and grilled bacon, ham or sausage. A stack of pancakes or a crisp waffle drenched in butter and syrup. Muffins or coffee cake, still warm from the oven. Hot buttered toast: white, wheat, rye or sourdough.

If you face a hard day's work, fortify yourself with eggs, bacon and potatoes, with a short stack of pancakes on the side. Or go the Spartan route of juice, black coffee and dry toast. In the diner, you're free to choose whatever you like, with nary a second glance from your server.

The range of breakfast choices presents a striking summary of our nation's immigrant past. Omelets and French toast from France, hash based on the corned beef of Irish and Jewish immigrants, Dutch waffles, the coffee cake's German streusel topping, New World blueberries and cornmeal in the muffins. Nowhere else and at no other time of day is the American melting pot more gloriously or abundantly displayed.

Buttermilk and Banana Waffles

Waffles were first prepared in France and Belgium during the Middle Ages. They were not introduced in America until centuries later, when Thomas Jefferson brought the first waffle iron home from France. Ripe bananas, added to this tangy buttermilk batter, produce moist, sweet results.

1   cup (5 oz/155 g) all-purpose (plain) flour
1   tablespoon sugar
1   teaspoon baking powder
½   teaspoon baking soda (bicarbonate of soda)
½   teaspoon ground cinnamon
¼   teaspoon salt
1¼ cups (10 fl oz/315 ml) buttermilk
1   egg
2   tablespoons unsalted butter, melted
2   ripe bananas, peeled and sliced
    Vegetable oil
    Maple syrup, warmed

❖ In a large bowl, stir together the flour, sugar, baking powder, baking soda, cinnamon and salt, mixing well.

❖ In a large measuring cup, combine the buttermilk, egg and melted butter and whisk until blended. Place half of the sliced bananas in a small bowl and mash coarsely; do not worry if the mixture is a little lumpy. Add the mashed banana to the buttermilk mixture, then stir into the flour mixture. Using a fork or whisk, mix until the batter is smooth.

❖ Preheat a waffle iron according to the manufacturer's directions. Using a paper towel or pastry brush, lightly grease the waffle iron with vegetable oil. Following the manufacturer's directions, ladle batter sufficient for 1 waffle into the iron, spreading it evenly. Close the waffle iron and cook until the waffle iron will open easily (no peeking for the first 2 minutes). Transfer the waffle to a platter and keep warm while you cook the remaining batter.

❖ Serve the waffles garnished with the remaining banana slices and drizzled with the warmed maple syrup.

Makes 7 waffles; serves 3 or 4

Sour Cream Pancakes

These lighter-than-air pancakes are perfect for topping with seasonal fruits, such as blueberries, boysenberries or nectarines. Out of season, use well-drained frozen fruit or even fruit preserves. A little grated lemon zest sprinkled over the top at the last minute makes a fresh and tangy garnish.

¾ cup (4 oz/125 g) all-purpose (plain) flour

¼ cup (¾ oz/20 g) quick-cooking rolled oats

1 tablespoon sugar

1 teaspoon baking powder

½ teaspoon baking soda (bicarbonate of soda)

½ teaspoon ground cinnamon

¼ teaspoon salt

½ cup (4 fl oz/125 ml) buttermilk

1 cup (8 fl oz/250 ml) sour cream

1 egg

2 tablespoons unsalted butter, melted

Vegetable oil

Blueberry or other fruit syrup, warmed

Fresh or frozen fruits or fruit preserves, optional *(see note)*

❖ In a large bowl, stir together the flour, rolled oats, sugar, baking powder, baking soda, cinnamon and salt, mixing well.

❖ In a large measuring cup, combine the buttermilk, sour cream, egg and melted butter. Using a fork, beat until well blended. Add the buttermilk mixture to the flour mixture and mix well with the fork or a whisk to form a smooth batter.

❖ Place a griddle or large nonstick frying pan over medium-high heat. When a drop of water sprinkled on top skitters across the surface, lightly grease the surface with vegetable oil.

❖ For each pancake, pour about ¼ cup (2 fl oz/60 ml) of the batter onto the hot surface; do not crowd the surface. Cook until little bubbles appear on the tops of the pancakes, 3–5 minutes. Using a spatula, turn them and cook on the second side until both sides are equally browned, 1–2 minutes longer. Transfer the pancakes to a platter and keep warm while you cook the remaining batter.

❖ To serve, drizzle the pancakes with warmed fruit syrup, garnish with fruit, if desired, and serve at once.

Makes about sixteen 4-inch (10-cm) pancakes; serves 4

Spanish Omelet

These omelets make a substantial breakfast or a hearty lunch. If hungry guests are standing by, serve each omelet as soon as it is done; if your crowd is more patient, wait until all are cooked to begin eating. Serve with a side of toast and potatoes O'Brien (recipe on page 13).

SAUCE
2   tablespoons olive oil
1   yellow onion, thinly sliced
½   green bell pepper (capsicum), seeded, deribbed and cut lengthwise into narrow strips
1   clove garlic, minced
2   cups (16 fl oz/500 ml) tomato sauce *(recipe on page 14)*
    Salt and freshly ground pepper

OMELETS
12 eggs
    Pinch of salt
    Pinch of freshly ground pepper
6   tablespoons (3 oz/90 g) unsalted butter
1¼ cups (5 oz/155 g) shredded Cheddar cheese

❖ To make the sauce, in a large non-stick frying pan over medium heat, warm the olive oil. Add the onion and sauté, stirring occasionally, until just beginning to soften, 3–4 minutes. Add the green pepper and continue to sauté, stirring occasionally, until the green pepper begins to soften, 3–4 minutes. Add the garlic and sauté for 1 minute longer. Then add the tomato sauce and simmer, stirring occasionally, until slightly reduced, about 3 minutes. Season to taste with salt and pepper, cover and keep warm.

❖ To make the omelets, in a bowl, whisk together the eggs, salt and pepper until well blended. In an 8-inch (20-cm) nonstick frying pan or omelet pan over medium heat, melt 1 tablespoon of the butter. When the foam subsides, add one-sixth of the beaten eggs and immediately stir the center with the flat side of a fork. Then, with the tines of the fork, lift the edges of the omelet and tilt the pan so that any uncooked egg runs underneath the cooked portion. Vigorously slide the pan back and forth over the burner until the omelet moves freely.

❖ When the omelet is lightly cooked but still creamy in the center, mound one-sixth of the cheese over half of the omelet. Using a spatula, lift and fold the uncovered half over the filling. Slide the omelet onto a warmed individual plate and spoon some of the sauce over the top. Cover lightly with aluminum foil and keep warm while you cook the remaining omelets.

❖ Serve the omelets piping hot.

Serves 6

Strawberry-Topped French Toast

French toast, known in France as pain perdu, *or "lost bread," was at one time a way to use up day-old bread. Although all types of bread now go into this breakfast classic, many diners still opt for day-old slices, relying on the egg and milk for moisture.*

¾ cup (7½ oz/235 g) strawberry preserves

½ cup (2 oz/60 g) strawberries, hulled

4 eggs

1½ cups (12 fl oz/375 ml) milk

1 teaspoon vanilla extract (essence)

½ teaspoon minced orange zest

1 tablespoon sugar

8 slices egg bread or sourdough bread

3 tablespoons unsalted butter

❖ In a blender, combine the strawberry preserves and the strawberries. Purée, scraping down the sides of the blender. Add water, if needed, to form a syrupy consistency. Set aside.

❖ In a bowl, whisk together the eggs, milk, vanilla, orange zest and sugar until well blended. Working in batches if necessary, arrange the bread slices in a single layer in a baking dish with 2-inch (5-cm) sides. Pour the egg mixture over the bread slices and then turn them to coat evenly. Let the bread stand for 5 minutes, or a little longer if you like custardy French toast.

❖ In a large nonstick frying pan over medium heat, melt 1½ tablespoons of the butter. When the foam subsides, add half of the bread slices in a single layer and cook the bread until golden brown on the first side, 2–4 minutes. Turn the slices and cook on the second side until golden, about 2 minutes longer. (For drier toasts, cook them for 1–2 minutes longer after they turn golden.) Transfer to warmed individual plates, cover lightly with aluminum foil and keep warm. Repeat with the remaining butter and bread.

❖ To serve, drizzle with the strawberry syrup and serve immediately.

Serves 4

Corned Beef Hash with Poached Eggs

This transformation for leftover meat gets its name from the French hacher, *"to chop." The dish had become so popular by the mid-19th century that the economical American eateries serving it were nicknamed hash houses. For red flannel hash, add 2 or 3 beets, cooked, peeled and cubed, with the corned beef.*

Salt to taste, plus 1 teaspoon salt
2½ lb (1.25 kg) white or red potatoes, peeled and cut into ½-inch (12-mm) cubes
3 cups (18 oz/560 g) cubed cooked corned beef (½-inch/12-mm cubes)
½ cup (4 fl oz/125 ml) heavy (double) cream
2 tablespoons finely chopped fresh parsley
1 teaspoon Worcestershire sauce
¼ teaspoon cayenne pepper
2 tablespoons vegetable oil
1 large yellow onion, finely chopped
8 eggs
Fresh parsley sprigs, optional
Freshly ground pepper

❖ Fill a large pot three-fourths full with water, salt it lightly and bring to a boil. Add the potatoes, return to a boil, and boil until nearly tender when pierced with a fork, 7–10 minutes. Drain well.

❖ In a large bowl, combine the boiled potatoes, corned beef, cream, parsley, Worcestershire sauce, ½ teaspoon of the salt and the cayenne pepper. Mix well.

❖ In a large nonstick frying pan over medium heat, warm the vegetable oil. Add the onion and sauté, stirring occasionally, until translucent, 4–5 minutes. Add the potato mixture and mix well to distribute the onions evenly. Spread the corned beef hash evenly in the pan. Cook, flattening the hash with a spatula occasionally, until a slight crust forms on the bottom, about 10 minutes. Run the spatula around the pan edge as necessary to prevent sticking. Turn the mixture over and continue cooking, stirring frequently to break up the hash, until crusty

and browned, 12–14 minutes longer. Remove from the heat, cover and keep warm.

❖ In a large frying pan with high sides and a tight-fitting lid (or 2 pans if the pan is not very large), bring a generous amount of water to a rolling boil. Add the remaining ½ teaspoon salt. Turn off the heat. Immediately crack the eggs and gently release them just above the surface of the water. Cover and leave undisturbed for about 3 minutes for runny yolks or 5 minutes for set yolks. Using a slotted spoon, transfer the eggs to a paper towel–lined plate to drain briefly.

❖ Spoon the hash out onto warmed small individual plates and top with the eggs. Garnish with parsley, if desired, season to taste with salt and pepper and serve immediately.

Serves 4

Streusel Coffee Cake

An ideal companion for your morning beverage, this cake takes its name from the German word that describes its casually "strewn" topping. Baking powder, used instead of yeast, makes it possible to prepare the coffee cake shortly before serving.

STREUSEL
½   cup (3½ oz/105 g) firmly packed light or dark brown sugar
½   cup (2½ oz/75 g) all-purpose (plain) flour
½   cup (2 oz/60 g) finely chopped walnuts
¼   cup (2 oz/60 g) unsalted butter, chilled

CAKE
2¼   cups (11 oz/345 g) all-purpose (plain) flour
1½   teaspoons ground cinnamon
½   teaspoon ground nutmeg
1   teaspoon baking powder
1   teaspoon baking soda (bicarbonate of soda)
½   teaspoon salt
½   cup (4 oz/125 g) unsalted butter, at room temperature
¾   cup (6 oz/185 g) firmly packed dark brown sugar
½   cup (4 oz/125 g) granulated sugar
3   eggs
1¼   cups (10 fl oz/315 ml) buttermilk mixed with 1 teaspoon vanilla extract (essence)
2   firm yet ripe pears, such as Bosc, Anjou or Comice, peeled, cored and coarsely chopped

❖ Preheat an oven to 350°F (180°C). Butter and flour a 9-by-13-inch (23-by-33-cm) baking pan. Set aside.

❖ To make the streusel, in a small bowl, combine the brown sugar, flour, walnuts and butter. Using 2 knives, your fingertips or a pastry blender, work the ingredients together until the mixture resembles large bread crumbs. Cover and refrigerate until ready to use.

❖ To make the cake, in a large bowl, sift together the flour, cinnamon, nutmeg, baking powder, baking soda and salt. In a large bowl, using an electric mixer set on high speed, beat the butter until light and fluffy. Gradually add the brown and granulated sugars, continuing to beat until very light, about 3 minutes. Add the eggs, one at a time, beating well after each addition.

❖ Reduce the mixer to low speed and gradually beat in the flour mixture alternately with the buttermilk, beating until just mixed.

❖ Pour the batter into the prepared pan. Scatter the chopped pears and the streusel mixture evenly over the top, then press them gently into the top of the batter.

❖ Bake until the top of the cake is firm, the streusel is crisp and bubbling and a wooden skewer inserted into the center comes out clean, 40–45 minutes.

❖ Transfer to a wire rack and let cool slightly in the pan. Cut into squares and serve warm.

Makes one 9-by-13-inch (23-by-33-cm) cake; serves 10–12

Blueberry Cornmeal Muffins

*Two ingredients native to America—blueberries and corn—give these morning
muffins bright color and agreeable sweetness. All-purpose flour ensures that the texture
remains tender, without diminishing the cornmeal's golden color or crunch.*

½   cup (4 oz/125 g) unsalted butter, at room temperature

¾   cup (6 oz/185 g) granulated sugar

2   eggs

1   teaspoon vanilla extract (essence)

2   teaspoons baking powder

¼   teaspoon salt

1½   cups (7½ oz/235 g) all-purpose (plain) flour

½   cup (4 fl oz/125 ml) milk

½   cup (2½ oz/75 g) yellow cornmeal

2½   cups (10 oz/315 g) blueberries

2   tablespoons firmly packed light or dark brown sugar

❖ Preheat an oven to 375°F (190°C). Generously butter twelve ½-cup (4-fl oz/125-ml) muffin-tin cups.

❖ In a large bowl, using an electric mixer set on high speed, beat the butter until light and fluffy. Gradually add the granulated sugar, continuing to beat until light, about 2 minutes. Add the eggs, one at a time, beating well after each addition. Beat in the vanilla, baking powder and salt.

❖ Using a rubber spatula, fold in half of the flour, then half of the milk. Repeat with the remaining flour, all of the cornmeal and the remaining milk, then fold in the blueberries.

❖ Spoon the batter into the prepared muffin cups, filling each cup two-thirds full and evenly distributing the blueberries. Sprinkle the brown sugar evenly over the tops.

❖ Bake until golden or a toothpick inserted into the center of a muffin comes out clean, 35–40 minutes. Transfer the pan to a rack and let cool for 15 minutes. Turn out the muffins onto the rack and serve warm or at room temperature.

❖ Wrap any cooled leftover muffins airtight and store at room temperature for up to 2 days.

Makes 12 muffins

Golden Raisin-Bran Muffins

*Some versions of this definitive diner muffin come out too dry, but soaking the
bran cereal in the liquid ingredients until fully plumped ensures a wonderfully moist texture.
For best results, select an unprocessed bran cereal such as All Bran or Bran Buds.*

2   eggs

⅓   cup (2½ oz/75 g) firmly packed light or dark brown sugar

½   cup (4 fl oz/125 ml) vegetable oil

2   cups (16 fl oz/500 ml) buttermilk

½   teaspoon salt

1½ cups (4 oz/125 g) wheat bran cereal *(see note)*

2¼ cups (11 oz/360 g) all-purpose (plain) flour

2   teaspoons baking soda (bicarbonate of soda)

¾   cup (4½ oz/140 g) golden raisins (sultanas)

❖ Preheat an oven to 400°F (200°C). Generously butter twelve ½-cup (4-fl oz/125-ml) muffin-tin cups.

❖ In a large bowl, combine the eggs, brown sugar, vegetable oil, buttermilk, salt and bran cereal. Using a wooden spoon, mix well. Let rest for at least 10 minutes or up to 1 hour to soften the bran.

❖ In another bowl, stir together the flour and baking soda. Add the flour mixture to the milk mixture, stirring until just combined. Do not overmix. Stir in the raisins.

❖ Spoon the batter into the prepared muffin cups, filling each cup two-thirds full. Bake until golden, about 20 minutes. Do not overcook.

❖ Transfer the pan to a rack and let cool for 15 minutes. Turn out the muffins onto the rack and serve warm or at room temperature.

❖ Wrap any cooled leftover muffins airtight and store at room temperature for up to 2 days.

Makes 12 muffins

Soups and Sandwiches

*T*ake a seat at the counter or slide into a booth of any diner around midday, and there's a good chance you'll see a lunch special clipped to a corner of the menu. "Soup and sandwich combo," it will say, offering a bowl of the day's soup and your choice of sandwich. Chances are good that the price will be so low that you'll be hard-pressed to pass up the bargain.

But it's not just the price alone. There's something inherently irresistible and comforting about the combination. Soup warms the body, satisfies the appetite and soothes the soul. Sandwiches, the original convenience food, are easy to eat and contain pleasing contrasts of tastes and textures. Taken together—with the soup first or, as you might have done in childhood, alternating spoonfuls and bites—they provide, in miraculously short order, the feeling that you've dined well.

With such pleasures in mind, the recipes in this chapter present a wide variety of soup and sandwich options, to be enjoyed alone or in any number of combinations. And don't limit these foods just to lunch: In your own kitchen, feel free to offer a combo special on the evening menu as well.

Split Pea Soup with Bacon

Although the authentic version of this cool-weather diner favorite is smooth and creamy, you can give your split pea soup a little texture by setting aside some of the mixture before puréeing, then stirring the two batches together. Serve with buttermilk biscuits (recipe on page 81), or garlic or Parmesan toasts.

2	tablespoons olive oil
1	yellow onion, finely chopped
1	celery stalk, thinly sliced
2	carrots, peeled and thinly sliced
1	clove garlic, minced
1¼	cups (9 oz/280 g) green split peas, rinsed
6	slices thick-cut bacon
7	cups (56 fl oz/1.75 l) water
1	bay leaf
¾	teaspoon salt
¼	teaspoon freshly ground pepper
1	tablespoon finely chopped fresh parsley

❖ In a large, heavy pot over medium heat, warm the olive oil. Add the onion and sauté until softened, 3–5 minutes. Add the celery and carrots and sauté until the carrots are tender, 2–3 minutes longer. Add the garlic and sauté for 1 minute longer.

❖ Add the split peas, bacon, water and bay leaf, raise the heat to high and bring to a simmer. Reduce the heat to medium-low, cover partially and cook, stirring occasionally and scraping the bottom of the pot to prevent scorching, until the peas are soft, about 1 hour.

❖ Remove the bacon and the bay leaf. Discard the bay leaf. Cut the bacon into small squares; set aside.

❖ Using a blender, a food processor fitted with the metal blade or a hand blender, purée the soup until smooth and creamy. If a food processor or blender was used, return the purée to the pot.

❖ Reheat the soup over medium heat, stirring occasionally, until very hot. Season to taste with the salt and pepper and stir in the reserved bacon. Ladle into warmed soup bowls; sprinkle the parsley over the tops. Serve immediately.

Serves 4–6

Stick-to-Your-Ribs Chili

What makes an authentic chili, especially in the American Southwest, causes many heated discussions: beans or no beans, ground meat or chunks, mild or hot and so on. In this version, you can replace the oil with bacon fat or lard for a more savory taste. Serve with warm corn bread (recipe on page 82).

5 tablespoons (2½ fl oz/75 ml) vegetable oil

4 lb (2 kg) beef chuck, coarsely ground (minced)

3 large yellow onions, finely chopped

2 fresh jalapeño chili peppers, seeded and finely chopped

8 cloves garlic, minced

2 tablespoons ground cumin

4 teaspoons ground oregano

2 teaspoons ground coriander

1 teaspoon ground cinnamon

½ cup (1½ oz/45 g) chili powder

2 cans (12 fl oz/375 ml each) beer

2 cups (16 fl oz/500 ml) beef stock

1 can (28 oz/875 g) crushed tomatoes, with juices

3 cans (15 oz/470 g each) kidney or pinto beans, drained

2 teaspoons salt

GARNISHES
Sour cream
Tomato salsa or jalapeño salsa
Shredded sharp Cheddar cheese
Chopped green (spring) onion
or red (Spanish) onion

❖ In a large nonstick frying pan over medium-high heat, warm 1 tablespoon of the vegetable oil. Add half of the meat and brown, stirring occasionally, until no pinkness remains, 5–7 minutes. Transfer to a colander placed over a bowl to drain off the fat. Brown the remaining meat in another tablespoon of the oil, then drain it. Set aside.

❖ In a 6-qt (6-l) pot over medium heat, warm the remaining 3 tablespoons oil. Add the onions and sauté, stirring occasionally, until softened, 5–8 minutes. Add the jalapeños and sauté for 1 minute longer. Add the garlic, cumin, oregano, coriander, cinnamon and chili powder and stir until combined. Cook for 1 minute longer.

❖ Add the reserved beef, the beer, beef stock and tomatoes and their juices and bring to a gentle simmer. Reduce the heat to medium-low, cover partially and simmer, stirring occasionally, for 1 hour.

❖ Stir in the beans and continue simmering, uncovered, until slightly thickened, about 30 minutes. Add the salt and stir until blended.

❖ To serve, ladle the chili into warmed individual bowls. Arrange small bowls of sour cream, salsa, Cheddar cheese and chopped onion alongside, for diners to add as desired.

Serves 10–12

Chicken Noodle Vegetable Soup

Leftover cooked chicken helps you put together this comforting bowlful in a hurry. You can vary the vegetables with the season, adding eggplant (aubergine), mushrooms, peas, green beans, broccoli, sliced tomatoes or whatever you like. For an authentic diner experience, serve with saltine crackers.

6   cups (48 fl oz/1.5 l) chicken stock
1   yellow onion, finely chopped
2   carrots, peeled, halved length-wise, and thinly sliced
2   celery stalks, thinly sliced
2   zucchini (courgettes), thinly sliced
2   tablespoons finely chopped fresh parsley
2   oz (60 g) dried very thin egg noodles
½   cup (3 oz/90 g) shredded or cubed, skinless cooked chicken meat
     Salt and freshly ground pepper

❖ In a large saucepan over medium-low heat, bring the chicken stock to a simmer. Add the onion, carrots and celery and continue to simmer until the vegetables are slightly soft, about 10 minutes. Add the zucchini and 1 tablespoon of the parsley and cook until the zucchini is just tender, about 10 minutes longer.

❖ Add the noodles and simmer until they are just tender, 3–4 minutes, or according to the package directions.

❖ Three minutes before the noodles are done, add the chicken and heat through. Season to taste with salt and pepper.

❖ Ladle into warmed soup bowls and sprinkle the tops with the remaining 1 tablespoon parsley. Serve immediately.

Serves 4

Grilled Hamburgers

Beef patty sandwiches have been eaten in America since the early 19th century, although it was not until the late 1920s that the White Castle chain popularized the hamburger as roadside diner fare. Garnish the burgers with mustard, catsup (tomato sauce) and pickle relish.

4   thick red (Spanish) onion slices
4   thick beefsteak tomato slices
1½ tablespoons fresh lemon juice
4   tablespoons olive oil
1⅓ lb (660 g) ground (minced) sirloin or chuck
½   teaspoon salt
¼   teaspoon freshly ground pepper
3   tablespoons bottled chili sauce, or to taste
¼   cup (2 fl oz/60 ml) ice water
4   large onion rolls or hamburger buns, split
¾   cup (2½ oz/75 g) shredded iceberg lettuce

❖ In a small bowl, combine the onion and tomato slices with the lemon juice and 3 tablespoons of the olive oil. Turn to coat evenly and set aside.

❖ Prepare a fire in a charcoal grill or preheat an indoor grill or broiler (griller). In a large bowl, combine the meat, salt, pepper, chili sauce and ice water. (The ice water helps to keep the burgers juicy.) Using a fork, stir together until well mixed. Then, using your hands, form the meat mixture into 4 patties each 1 inch (2.5 cm) thick, being careful not to handle the meat too much. Set aside.

❖ Place the onion rolls or hamburger buns, cut side down, on the grill rack or a broiler pan; grill or broil until just golden, 2–3 minutes. Transfer to individual plates, cut side up, and brush the remaining 1 tablespoon olive oil lightly over the toasted buns.

❖ Position the grill or broiler rack 4 inches (10 cm) from the heat source, then grill or broil the burgers, turning once, for 6 minutes on the first side and 4–5 minutes on the second side for medium-rare to medium.

❖ Place each burger on the bottom half of the toasted bun, top with a slice each of red onion and tomato, and sprinkle with a little of the lettuce. Cover with the top bun and serve immediately.

Serves 4

Tuna Melt

Tuna salad, Cheddar cheese and sourdough bread—three of the best foods in life—come together in a single grilled sandwich. For a more luxurious version, substitute fresh or canned crab meat for the tuna. Serve with potato salad (recipe on page 89) or tricolor coleslaw (page 86).

1 can (12¼ oz/382 g) water-packed white albacore tuna, drained
1 celery stalk, finely diced
2 tablespoons minced fresh parsley
2 tablespoons sweet green pickle relish
1 teaspoon fresh lemon juice
½ cup (4 oz/125 ml) mayonnaise
4 thick slices sourdough bread
1 cup (4 oz/125 g) shredded sharp Cheddar cheese
4 lemon wedges
4 fresh parsley sprigs

❖ Preheat a broiler (griller).

❖ In a bowl, combine the tuna, celery, parsley, pickle relish, lemon juice and mayonnaise. Toss with a fork until well mixed.

❖ Place the bread slices on a broiler pan. Divide the tuna mixture evenly among them, mounding it slightly. Sprinkle the cheese evenly over the tuna mixture.

❖ Place under the broiler and broil (grill) until the tops just begin to bubble and are golden, 3–4 minutes. Watch carefully or the cheese may brown too much.

❖ Transfer to individual plates and garnish with a lemon wedge and a parsley sprig. Serve immediately.

Serves 4

Reuben Sandwich

A New York City restaurant called Reuben's first produced this classic sandwich. If you like, substitute pastrami for the corned beef. Make sure to squeeze the sauerkraut dry to avoid a soggy sandwich. Serve with a side of beer-battered onion rings (recipe on page 85) or pickle chips.

8 slices rye bread with caraway
   seeds

¼ cup (2 oz/60 g) unsalted butter,
   at room temperature

¾ cup (6 fl oz/180 ml) Thousand
   Island dressing *(recipe on page 57)*

¼ lb (125 g) corned beef, thinly
   sliced

1 cup (6 oz/185 g) well-drained
   sauerkraut

½ lb (250 g) Swiss cheese,
   shredded

❖ On a large work surface, lay out the bread slices. Spread one side of each slice evenly with the butter. Turn the slices over and spread the other side evenly with the dressing.

❖ Lay the sliced corned beef on the dressing-spread side of 4 of the bread slices, tucking in any overhang. Spread the sauerkraut evenly atop the corned beef, then distribute the cheese evenly over the sauerkraut. Top with the remaining bread slices, buttered side out, and press down firmly to compact the sandwiches.

❖ Heat a large nonstick frying pan or a griddle until hot. Working in batches if necessary and using a spatula, carefully transfer the sandwiches to the hot pan or griddle.

Cook, pressing down gently on each sandwich with the spatula 3 or 4 times, until golden on the first side, 4–5 minutes. Carefully turn over the sandwiches and cook, again pressing down on them, until the second side is golden and the cheese has melted, 3–4 minutes longer. Turn over one more time and cook 2–3 minutes longer.

❖ Transfer to individual plates and serve immediately.

Serves 4

Triple-Decker Club Sandwich

Whether it had its origins in elite country clubs or in the club cars of passenger trains, this sandwich has long been a diner standby across America. Variations abound, but turkey and bacon are the traditional fillings; other meats such as ham or smoked chicken may be included, and avocado makes a nice addition.

12 slices white bread
16 slices thick-cut bacon
⅓ cup (3 fl oz/80 ml) mayonnaise
2 teaspoons fresh lemon juice
¼ teaspoon salt
  Pinch of white pepper
½ lb (250 g) cooked turkey breast, thinly sliced
2 tomatoes, sliced
8 large iceberg lettuce leaves, torn into pieces

❖ Toast the bread slices until golden brown. Set aside.

❖ In a large nonstick frying pan over medium heat, cook the bacon, turning once, until crisp, 4–6 minutes. Transfer to a plate lined with a double thickness of paper towels and set aside.

❖ In a small bowl, stir together the mayonnaise, lemon juice, salt and white pepper, mixing well.

❖ Assemble the bacon, lemon mayonnaise, turkey, tomatoes and lettuce around a large work surface before you begin to make the sandwiches.

❖ Lay the bread slices on the work surface and spread them evenly with the lemon mayonnaise. Top 4 of the bread slices with an equal amount of the turkey, followed by half of the lettuce. Top the lettuce with a second slice of bread, mayonnaise side up.

Place an equal number of tomato slices and then 4 bacon slices on each sandwich, and top with the remaining lettuce. Place the 4 remaining bread slices, mayonnaise side down, on top. Press down gently to compact the sandwiches and secure them with toothpicks.

❖ To serve, using a serrated knife, slice into halves or quarters, then transfer to individual plates.

Serves 4

Grilled Cheese Sandwich

The grilled cheese sandwich is America's simple take on a dish that appears in the cuisines of many different countries, from the croque-monsieur in France to Mexico's quesadilla. For a variation, add thinly sliced turkey or ham or substitute any good melting cheese for one or both of the cheeses.

1   cup (4 oz/125 g) shredded sharp Cheddar cheese

1   cup (4 oz/125 g) shredded Monterey Jack cheese

8   slices sourdough bread

¼   cup (2 oz/60 g) unsalted butter, at room temperature

1½ tablespoons Dijon-style mustard

8   thick tomato slices

❖ In a bowl, combine the cheeses and mix until blended. Set aside.

❖ On a large work surface, lay out the bread slices and spread them evenly with the butter. Then turn them buttered-side down on the surface and spread the other side thinly with the mustard.

❖ Sprinkle half of the cheese mixture evenly onto the mustard-spread side of 4 of the slices. Lay 2 tomato slices atop each cheese-topped slice and then sprinkle the remaining cheese evenly over the tomatoes. Top the sandwiches with the remaining 4 slices of bread, mustard side down, and press down gently to compact the sandwiches.

❖ Heat a large nonstick frying pan or griddle to medium heat. Working in batches if necessary and using a spatula, carefully transfer the sandwiches to the hot pan or griddle. Cook, pressing down gently on each sandwich with the spatula 3 or 4 times, until golden and slightly crusty on the first side, 3–4 minutes. Carefully turn over the sandwiches and continue cooking, again pressing down on them, until the second side is golden and the cheese has begun to ooze out the sides slightly, 2–3 minutes longer.

❖ Transfer to individual plates and serve immediately.

Serves 4

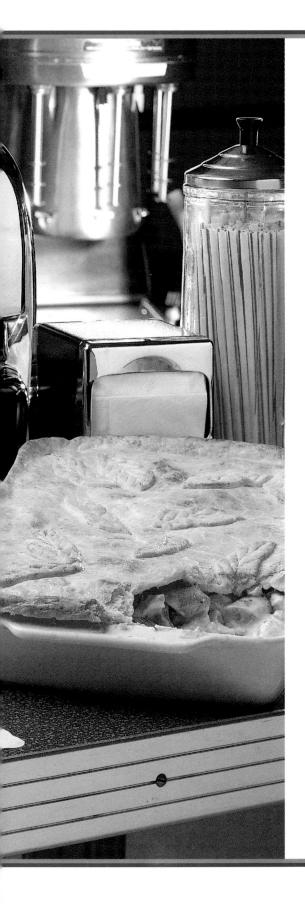

Blue Plate Specials

*H*istory isn't clear on where or when diners first started serving the day's main-course special on blue plates that stood out from the other tableware. But the term *blue plate special* came to signify good value for money: a home-style dish of meat or poultry, joined by potatoes and one or two vegetables. Often, the price of the special also included your choice of soup or salad and a dessert.

The recipes that follow provide you with the centerpiece of that blue plate special. Reflecting the humble, wholly satisfying philosophy behind this diner tradition, the recipes feature reasonably priced ingredients such as ground beef, pork chops and turkey breast, given full flavor through imaginative seasoning and slow, simple cooking. You'll also find options for salad lovers, as well as pasta favorites from the children's menu.

It's easy to complete your own blue plate special. Start with one of the soups from the preceding chapter, or a salad of crisp greens. Serve the main course with any of your favorite side dishes (pages 78–97) and potatoes (pages 12–13). Finish with any of the desserts at the end of this book, and you'll have joined the ranks of diners everywhere offering satisfying meals prepared at bargain prices.

Chef's Salad

Although the chef's salad originated as a way for frugal cooks to use up leftover ingredients, this diner favorite has long since evolved into a featured dish on its own. The salad will look best if the meats and cheeses are all cut into strips of nearly uniform size, about ⅜ inch (1 cm) wide and 2 inches (5 cm) long.

VINAIGRETTE
2 tablespoons fresh lemon juice
2 teaspoons Dijon-style mustard
1 teaspoon finely minced shallot
Salt and freshly ground pepper
¼ cup (2 fl oz/60 ml) vegetable oil
2 tablespoons extra-virgin olive oil

SALAD
2 heads butter lettuce, pale inner leaves only, carefully washed and dried
⅓ lb (155 g) honey-baked ham, cut into julienne strips
⅓ lb (155 g) smoked chicken or roast turkey, cut into julienne strips
½ lb (250 g) Monterey Jack or Swiss cheese, cut into julienne strips
8 red or yellow cherry tomatoes, cut into quarters
3 hard-cooked eggs, cut into quarters

❖ To make the vinaigrette, in a small bowl, whisk together the lemon juice, mustard, shallot, and salt and pepper to taste. Slowly pour in the vegetable and olive oils, whisking continuously. Continue whisking for another 10–20 seconds until emulsified. Set aside.

❖ To make the salad, tear any larger lettuce leaves into bite-sized pieces; leave the smaller leaves whole. Place the lettuce in a large salad bowl or 4 individual salad bowls. Arrange the ham, chicken or turkey, and cheese on top, keeping each ingredient separate and radiating the strips outward from the center of the bowl. Place the tomato and egg wedges in between the meats and cheese.

❖ Serve the salad with the vinaigrette on the side, then dress and toss at the table.

Serves 4

Seafood Louis

This California specialty of seafood atop fresh greens is defined, in part, by its creamy Thousand Island dressing. If you wish, you can use either all shrimp or all crab meat, or even substitute another cooked shellfish such as scallops or lobster.

THOUSAND ISLAND DRESSING
⅔ cup (5 fl oz/160 ml) mayonnaise
⅓ cup (2½ fl oz/80 ml) bottled chili sauce
2 tablespoons sweet green pickle relish
Salt and freshly ground pepper

SALAD
1 head iceberg lettuce, shredded (about 8 cups/1½ lb/750 g)
¼ English (hothouse) cucumber, thinly sliced
½ lb (250 g) fresh-cooked lump crab meat, picked over for cartilage and shell fragments
½ lb (250 g) cooked tiny shrimp (prawns)
1 ripe avocado, pitted, peeled and sliced
2 hard-cooked eggs, cut into quarters
8 red or yellow cherry tomatoes
1 tablespoon finely chopped fresh parsley
1 lemon, cut into wedges

❖ To make the dressing, in a small bowl, stir together the mayonnaise, chili sauce, pickle relish, and salt and pepper to taste. You will have about 1 cup (8 fl oz/250 ml). Cover and refrigerate until needed.

❖ To make the salad, in a large salad bowl or 4 individual salad bowls, combine the lettuce and cucumber and toss to mix. Mound the crab meat and the shrimp in the center of the bowl(s) and arrange the avocado slices, egg quarters and tomatoes around the seafood.

❖ Spoon the dressing over the seafood and garnish with the parsley. Toss at the table and pass the lemon wedges for squeezing over the top.

Serves 4

Macaroni and Cheese

Although the pasta tubes known as macaroni came from Italy more than two hundred years ago, baking them with a cheese sauce became popular in America only in the 19th century. Try adding different varieties of Cheddar or other melting cheeses, small ham cubes, or finely sliced fresh basil.

MACARONI
1   teaspoon salt
2½   cups (9 oz/280 g) dried elbow macaroni
1   tablespoon vegetable oil or olive oil

SAUCE
3   tablespoons unsalted butter
3   tablespoons all-purpose (plain) flour
2½   cups (20 fl oz/625 ml) milk, warmed
1¾   cups (7 oz/220 g) shredded sharp Cheddar cheese
½   teaspoon salt
½   teaspoon freshly ground pepper
2   teaspoons Dijon-style mustard
1   teaspoon finely chopped fresh parsley

TOPPING
¾   cup (3 oz/90 g) shredded sharp Cheddar cheese
½   cup (1 oz/30 g) fresh bread crumbs
1   teaspoon unsalted butter, cut into tiny pieces

❖ Preheat an oven to 375°F (190°C). Butter an 8-inch (20-cm) square baking pan or dish.

❖ For the macaroni, bring a large saucepan three-fourths full of water to a rapid boil. Add the salt and the macaroni and stir to separate. Cook, stirring occasionally, until al dente, 5–7 minutes, or according to package directions. Drain and rinse with cool water to remove any excess starch. Place in a large mixing bowl and drizzle with the oil. Set aside.

❖ To make the sauce, in a saucepan over medium-low heat, melt the butter. Sprinkle the flour over the butter and whisk constantly until the flour is absorbed and the mixture is gently bubbling and lightly golden, 2–3 minutes. Gradually add the warm milk, whisking continuously, and bring to a simmer. Continue to simmer, stirring, until smooth and slightly thickened, 3–4 minutes.

❖ Add the 1¾ cups (7 oz/220 g) cheese to the milk mixture, remove from the heat and whisk constantly until the cheese melts. Stir in the salt, pepper, mustard and parsley. Pour the sauce over the macaroni and mix to combine. Transfer the macaroni to the prepared baking pan.

❖ To make the topping, in a small bowl, stir together the cheese and bread crumbs. Sprinkle evenly over the macaroni. Dot with the butter.

❖ Bake until the top bubbles and begins to form a crust, 20–25 minutes; cover the top with aluminum foil if it begins to brown too much. Remove from the oven and let stand for about 5 minutes before serving.

Serves 4

Old-fashioned Meat Loaf

For the most tender, moist meat loaf, use meat with 20 percent fat. A meat loaf pan—a wonderful recent invention consisting of one pan with drainage holes set inside a second pan—allows excess fat to drain out during cooking. Serve with a generous helping of mashed potatoes (recipe on page 12).

2   tablespoons vegetable oil
1   large yellow onion, chopped
1   carrot, peeled and finely chopped
2   cloves garlic, minced
2   lb (1 kg) lean ground (minced) beef
1½ cups (3 oz/90 g) fresh bread crumbs
2   eggs, lightly beaten
1   teaspoon salt
½   teaspoon freshly ground pepper
¼   teaspoon dried thyme leaves, crumbled
¼   cup finely chopped fresh parsley
1   tablespoon Worcestershire sauce
⅔   cup (5 fl oz/160 ml) catsup (tomato sauce)
½   cup (4 fl oz/125 ml) tomato sauce *(recipe on page 14)*, plus tomato sauce for serving, optional

❖ In a nonstick frying pan over medium heat, warm the vegetable oil. Add the onion and carrot and sauté, stirring occasionally, until the carrot begins to soften and the onion is almost translucent, 4–5 minutes. Add the garlic and sauté for 1 minute longer. Remove from the heat and set aside to cool.

❖ Preheat an oven to 350°F (180°C). Lightly oil a 9-by-5-by-3-inch (23-by-13-by-7.5-cm) loaf pan.

❖ In a large bowl, combine the beef, bread crumbs and the cooled vegetable mixture. In a medium bowl, whisk together the eggs, salt, pepper, thyme, parsley, Worcestershire sauce and catsup until combined. Pour the egg mixture over the beef mixture. Using your hands, mix the ingredients together, handling just enough to combine evenly. Do not overmix or the loaf will be too compact and dry.

❖ Pat the meat mixture gently into the prepared loaf pan; don't press too firmly. Pour the ½ cup (4 fl oz/125 ml) tomato sauce evenly over the top. Bake until the loaf has begun to shrink from the sides of the pan and an instant-read thermometer inserted into the center registers 150°F (66°C), about 1¼ hours. Transfer to a rack and let cool for 10 minutes.

❖ Cut the meat loaf into thick slices and, using a spatula, lift out of the pan and place on warmed individual plates. Serve warm or cold, accompanied with more of the tomato sauce, if desired.

Serves 6

Roast Turkey with Mashed Potatoes and Gravy

Smart diner cooks know that a simply roasted turkey breast can make any day feel like a holiday. In this recipe, a marinade helps keep the meat juicy, while adding extra flavor. Ask your butcher to bone the breast for you, then to roll and tie it for more even cooking.

¼ cup (2 fl oz/60 ml) olive oil

1 clove garlic, minced

1 teaspoon dried thyme, crumbled

1 teaspoon dried sage, crumbled

⅛ teaspoon freshly ground pepper, plus pepper to taste

1 boneless turkey breast, about 3¼ lb (1.6 kg), rolled and tied
Salt

2 cups (16 fl oz/500 ml) chicken stock

GRAVY

½ cup (4 fl oz/125 ml) water

2 tablespoons unsalted butter

2 tablespoons all-purpose (plain) flour

1 cup (8 fl oz/250 ml) chicken stock, warmed
Salt and freshly ground pepper

Mashed potatoes *(recipe on page 12)*

❖ In a large baking dish, stir together the olive oil, garlic, thyme, sage and the ⅛ teaspoon pepper. Place the turkey breast in the dish and rub the mixture over the entire surface of the turkey breast. Cover and refrigerate overnight, basting a few times with the marinade.

❖ Preheat the oven to 350°F (180°C).

❖ Place the breast on a rack in a roasting pan, season lightly with salt and pepper and pour 1 cup (8 fl oz/ 250 ml) of the chicken stock over the breast and into the bottom of the pan. Roast, basting with the pan juices every 5–10 minutes, until an instant-read thermometer inserted into the center registers 165°F (74°C), about 1 hour and 20 minutes. Check the pan periodically during roasting and add the remaining 1 cup (8 fl oz/250 ml) stock to the pan as it becomes dry. Transfer the breast to a warmed serving platter and cover with aluminum foil while you make the gravy.

❖ To make the gravy, place the roasting pan on the stove top over high heat, add the water and deglaze the pan by stirring to dislodge any browned bits on the pan bottom. Boil until the liquid is reduced by half, about 2 minutes. Remove from the heat and set aside.

❖ In a saucepan over medium heat, melt the butter. Sprinkle the flour over the butter and whisk constantly until the flour is absorbed and the mixture is bubbling and golden, 2–3 minutes. Add the reduced drippings and warmed chicken stock and continue to whisk until thickened, 7–10 minutes. Season to taste with salt and pepper.

❖ Snip and discard the string from the turkey breast. Slice the meat and serve on warmed individual plates. Place a mound of mashed potatoes alongside and drizzle the gravy over the turkey and potatoes.

Serves 6

Chicken Pot Pie

Although simple pastry-topped meat stews originated long ago in England, the humble meat pie has been satisfying American appetites only since the late 18th century. This recipe uses baby vegetables and boneless chicken breasts to turn out a great pie in record time.

CHEDDAR PASTRY

2 cups (10 oz/315 g) all-purpose (plain) flour

¾ cup (6 oz/185 g) unsalted butter, chilled, cut into small pieces

1 cup (4 oz/125 g) shredded sharp Cheddar cheese

½ cup (4 fl oz/125 ml) ice water

FILLING

2¼ cups (18 fl oz/560 ml) chicken stock

2 skinless, boneless whole chicken breasts, about 1½ lb (750 g) total
Salt

2½ cups (12 oz/375 g) baby carrots, cut into 1-inch (2.5-cm) pieces

3 celery stalks, thickly sliced

10 oz (315 g) pearl onions, peeled *(see glossary, page 126)*

1 cup (5 oz/155 g) small peas

6 tablespoons (3 oz/90 g) unsalted butter

7 tablespoons (2½ oz/75 g) all-purpose (plain) flour

1 cup (8 fl oz/250 ml) heavy (double) cream
Salt and freshly ground pepper

1 teaspoon minced fresh thyme

3 tablespoons snipped fresh chives

3 tablespoons minced fresh parsley

1 egg, lightly beaten

❖ To make the Cheddar pastry, place the flour in a bowl. Using a pastry blender or your fingertips, work in the butter until crumbly. Add the cheese and work in until just blended. Sprinkle the ice water over the pastry dough, a little at a time, and gather the pastry into a ball. Knead lightly until just combined. Wrap in plastic wrap and chill until needed.

❖ To make the filling, in a saucepan over medium heat, bring the stock to a simmer. Add the chicken and simmer, uncovered, until opaque throughout, 15–20 minutes. Remove from the heat and let the chicken cool completely in the liquid. Remove the breasts, reserving the stock. You should have about 2½ cups (20 fl oz/625 ml) stock. Cut the chicken into ¾-inch (2-cm) chunks. Set aside.

❖ Bring a saucepan three-fourths full of water to a boil and salt lightly. Add the carrots and cook over medium-high heat for 5–6 minutes. Add the celery, pearl onions and peas and cook until all are barely tender, about 3 minutes longer. Drain well; set aside.

❖ In a saucepan over medium heat, melt the butter. Sprinkle in the flour and whisk until the mixture is gently bubbling and smooth, 2–3 minutes; do not brown. Gradually add the reserved stock, whisking constantly, and bring to a simmer. Cook, stirring often, until smooth and slightly thickened, 4–5 minutes. Add the cream and cook, stirring occasionally, until the sauce coats the back of the spoon, about 5 minutes longer. Remove from the heat and stir in the salt and pepper to taste, the thyme, chives and parsley.

❖ Preheat an oven to 400°F (200°C). Add the chicken and vegetables to the sauce and stir to combine. Spoon into a 9-by-13-inch (23-by-33-cm) baking dish. Brush the edge of the dish with some of the beaten egg.

❖ On a lightly floured work surface, roll out the pastry into a rectangle 10 by 15 inches (25 by 38 cm). Transfer the pastry to the dish, pressing on the edges firmly. Trim away the overhang. Gently knead the dough scraps together, roll out ⅛ inch (3 mm) thick and cut out several small leaf shapes. Brush the top of the pie with the beaten egg. Using the knife, score the pastry leaves lightly, attach them to the pie pastry, and brush with more egg. Cut 3 slits each 1 inch (2.5 cm) long at the center of the pie.

❖ Bake until golden, 25–30 minutes. Remove from the oven and let stand for 5 minutes, then spoon onto warmed individual plates or bowls.

Serves 8

Fried Chicken

One of the South's greatest contributions to American cooking, fried chicken gained nationwide popularity in the early 20th century and has been a diner favorite ever since. Serve hot with mashed potatoes (recipe on page 12) or at room temperature with potato salad (page 89).

1	chicken, 3½–4 lb (1.75–2 kg), cut into 8 serving pieces
1½	cups (12 fl oz/375 ml) buttermilk
3	teaspoons salt
½	teaspoon freshly ground black pepper
½	teaspoon paprika
¼	teaspoon cayenne pepper
2	cups (10 oz/315 g) all-purpose (plain) flour
3–4	cups (1½–2 lb/750 g–1 kg) vegetable shortening

❖ Rinse the chicken pieces and blot dry with paper towels. In a large bowl, combine the buttermilk, 1 teaspoon of the salt, ¼ teaspoon each of the black pepper and paprika and ⅛ teaspoon of the cayenne pepper. Add the chicken pieces and turn to coat evenly. Cover and refrigerate for at least 2 hours or as long as overnight, turning the pieces occasionally.

❖ In a pie plate, combine the flour and the remaining 2 teaspoons salt, ¼ teaspoon each black pepper and paprika and ⅛ teaspoon cayenne. Stir well with a fork.

❖ Line a baking sheet with 3 layers of paper towels and place it near the stove. Put the shortening in a large cast-iron frying pan or heavy pot and melt over medium-high heat. The shortening should be about 1½ inches (4 cm) deep. Heat until it registers 365°F (185°C) on a deep-fat frying thermometer, or until a small cube of bread dropped into the oil browns in about 1 minute.

❖ Using tongs, remove the chicken thighs from the marinade, draining well. Dredge them in the flour mixture, turning to coat evenly, and shake off the excess flour. Place the thighs, skin side down, in the center of the pan. Coat the remaining chicken pieces in the same way and add them to the pan in a single layer.

❖ Do not move the chicken until the coating is set and looks firm, 4–6 minutes. Check the underside by lifting with tongs; it should be deep golden brown. Turn over and fry on the second side until also deep golden brown, rotating the pieces as necessary. Remove from the pan when done, 17–20 minutes for breasts and 20–25 minutes for the other pieces. To test, cut into the thickest part of a piece; the juices should run clear and the meat should be opaque throughout. Place on the towel-lined baking sheet to drain. If you want to serve hot, cover and keep warm until all the chicken is cooked.

❖ Arrange the chicken pieces on a platter or individual plates and serve hot, at room temperature or cold.

Serves 4–6

Double-Thick Apple-Stuffed Pork Chops

A small pocket, cut in the center of double-thick pork chops, makes a perfect receptacle for herbed sautéed apples and bread crumbs. If double-thick chops are not available at your market, ask your butcher to cut them for you. Serve with creamed spinach (recipe on page 90).

3 tablespoons olive oil

½ cup finely chopped yellow onion

½ firm green apple, peeled, cored and finely chopped

¼ teaspoon ground sage

1 cup (4 oz/125 g) fine dried bread crumbs

2 tablespoons plus 1¼ cups (10 fl oz/300 ml) apple cider
 Salt and freshly ground pepper

4 double-thick pork chops, about ¾ lb (375 g) each

½ cup (4 fl oz/125 ml) beef stock

¼ cup (2 fl oz/60 ml) heavy (double) cream

2 tablespoons finely chopped fresh parsley

❖ In a small frying pan over medium heat, warm 1 tablespoon of the olive oil. Add the onion and sauté until almost translucent, 3–4 minutes. Add the apple and sauté until almost tender, 2–3 minutes. Transfer to a bowl and add the sage, bread crumbs and the 2 tablespoons apple cider. Stir well. Season to taste with salt and pepper.

❖ Using a small, sharp knife, cut a horizontal slit 1 inch (2.5 cm) long into the side of each pork chop. Then, working inward from the slit, cut almost to the opposite side of the chop; be careful not to cut through the chop completely.

❖ Spoon an equal amount of the apple mixture into the pocket of each chop. Secure with toothpicks.

❖ Preheat an oven to 375°F (190°C). In a large nonstick frying pan over medium-high heat, warm the remaining 2 tablespoons olive oil. Using tongs, place the pork chops in the pan and brown, turning once, until golden on both sides, 3–4 minutes. (Push down the toothpicks when turning the chops over.)

❖ Carefully transfer the pork chops to a roasting pan large enough to hold them close together in a single layer. Reserve the frying pan. Pour ¾ cup (6 fl oz/180 ml) of the apple cider around the chops. Cover the pan with aluminum foil and bake for 15 minutes. Remove the foil and continue to bake until the chops are well browned and cooked through, about 10 minutes longer.

❖ Transfer the pork chops to a warmed serving platter, remove and discard the toothpicks, and cover with aluminum foil to keep warm. Pour the juices from the roasting pan into a clean container and set aside.

❖ Place the reserved frying pan over medium-high heat. When the pan is hot, pour in the beef stock and the remaining ½ cup (4 fl oz/120 ml) apple cider and deglaze the pan by stirring to dislodge any browned bits from the pan bottom. Bring to a boil, and boil until the liquid is reduced by one-third, 2–3 minutes. Add the cream and swirl into the sauce. Reduce the heat to medium and simmer until the sauce thickens slightly and coats the back of a spoon, about 2 minutes longer. Add the reserved pan juices and season to taste with the salt and pepper.

❖ Spoon the sauce over the pork chops, sprinkle with the parsley and serve immediately.

Serves 4

BLUE PLATE SPECIALS

Pot Roast

As with most slowly braised dishes, this pot roast will taste best if left to cool, then refrigerated overnight and reheated before serving. Remove any excess fat from the surface of the chilled meat before serving. The amount of fat will depend, in part, upon the cut of your brisket; first (or flat) cut is the leanest. Serve with herbed and buttered noodles.

1 beef brisket, 4 lb (2 kg), preferably first cut
4 tablespoons (2 fl oz/60 ml) olive oil
2 yellow onions, coarsely chopped
2 slices bacon, cut into ½-inch (12-mm) pieces
2 carrots, peeled and thinly sliced
2 cups (16 fl oz/500 ml) beef stock
¾ cup (6 fl oz/180 ml) dry red wine
2 tablespoons red wine vinegar
1 clove garlic, minced
1 fresh thyme sprig or ½ teaspoon dried thyme, crumbled
3 fresh parsley sprigs
1 bay leaf
1 teaspoon salt, plus salt to taste
½ teaspoon freshly ground pepper, plus pepper to taste

❖ Pat the brisket dry with paper towels. In a large, heavy nonstick pot over medium-high heat, warm 2 tablespoons of the olive oil. Add the beef and brown evenly on all sides, 10–15 minutes. Transfer the beef to a dish.

❖ Add the remaining 2 tablespoons oil to the pot, along with the onions and bacon. Sauté over medium-high heat, stirring often, until the onions are browned and slightly caramelized, 12–15 minutes. Add the carrots and sauté until slightly softened, about 3 minutes longer.

❖ Add the beef stock, wine, vinegar, garlic, thyme, parsley and bay leaf and bring to a boil. Return the beef to the pot, reduce the heat to medium-low, cover partially and simmer until the meat is tender, 2–2½ hours. Maintain the heat so that the liquid barely simmers, and turn the roast several times during cooking.

❖ Transfer the roast to a cutting board, cover with aluminum foil and let rest for 15 minutes. Remove the bay leaf and herb sprigs and discard.

❖ Using a blender, a food processor fitted with the metal blade or a hand blender, purée the sauce. If using a blender or processor, return the sauce to the pot. Simmer the sauce over medium heat until slightly thickened, about 10 minutes. Add the 1 teaspoon salt and the ½ teaspoon pepper, then taste and adjust the seasoning.

❖ Cut the meat across the grain into thin slices. Arrange the slices on a warmed platter, overlapping them slightly, and spoon some of the sauce over the top. Serve any remaining sauce in a bowl on the side.

Serves 6

Beef Stew with Winter Vegetables

Butternut squash is added to this thick, meaty stew for sweetness and its natural thickening ability. Refrigerating the stew overnight will further improve the flavor, while making it easier to remove excess fat. Buttermilk biscuits (recipe on page 81) and parslied rice make perfect accompaniments.

½   cup (2½ oz/75 g) all-purpose (plain) flour

3   lb (1.5 kg) beef chuck, cut into 1½-inch (4-cm) cubes

5   tablespoons (3 fl oz/80 ml) olive oil

¼   cup (2 fl oz/60 ml) red wine vinegar

2   large yellow onions, thinly sliced

2   carrots, peeled and thinly sliced

2   cups (16 fl oz/500 ml) beef stock

1   cup (8 fl oz/250 ml) dry red wine

¼   cup (2 fl oz/60 ml) tomato paste

2   cloves garlic, minced

1   bay leaf

4   fresh parsley sprigs

1   fresh sage sprig or ½ teaspoon dried sage, crumbled

1   lb (500 g) butternut (pumpkin) squash, peeled, seeded and cut into bite-sized chunks

10   oz (315 g) pearl onions, peeled fresh *(see glossary, page 126)* or thawed frozen

½   teaspoon salt

¼   teaspoon freshly ground pepper

1   tablespoon finely chopped fresh parsley

❖ Spread the flour on a large plate. Coat the beef with the flour and shake off the excess.

❖ In a large, heavy nonstick pot over medium-high heat, warm 4 tablespoons (2 fl oz/60 ml) of the olive oil. Working in batches if necessary, add the beef and brown evenly on all sides, 5–7 minutes. Using tongs or a slotted spoon, transfer the beef to a plate.

❖ Add the vinegar to the pot and deglaze over medium-high heat by stirring to dislodge any browned bits from the pot bottom. Add the remaining 1 tablespoon oil and the yellow onions and cook over medium-high heat, stirring occasionally, until nicely browned, about 15 minutes.

❖ Add the carrots to the pot and sauté until slightly softened, about 3 minutes. Then add the beef stock, wine, tomato paste, garlic, bay leaf, parsley and sage. Reduce the heat to medium-low, cover and simmer, stirring occasionally, until the meat is almost tender, 1½–1¾ hours.

❖ Add the butternut squash, cover and continue to simmer until both the squash and meat are tender when pierced with a fork, about 15 minutes. Add the pearl onions and cook until just tender, about 5 minutes longer. Stir in the salt, pepper and parsley.

❖ Spoon onto warmed individual plates or bowls and serve immediately.

Serves 6

Barbecue-Style Braised Short Ribs

Beef short ribs are a highly flavorful cut, and slow cooking makes the meat so tender it almost falls off the bone. Parboiling the meat before cooking reduces the fat while retaining flavor. Serve with thick pieces of corn bread (recipe on page 82) or a generous helping of candied yams (page 94).

5   lb (2.5 kg) lean beef short ribs, cut into 3–4-inch (7.5–10-cm) pieces

1   teaspoon salt, plus salt to taste

½   teaspoon freshly ground pepper, plus pepper to taste

2   tablespoons vegetable oil

2   yellow onions, thickly sliced crosswise into rings

2   carrots, peeled and sliced

4   cloves garlic, coarsely chopped

2   cups (16 fl oz/500 ml) tomato sauce *(recipe on page 14)*

1   cup (8 fl oz/250 ml) bottled barbecue sauce

1   cup (8 fl oz/250 ml) beef stock

❖ Bring a large pot three-fourths full of water to a boil. Plunge the short ribs into the water, cover partially and parboil for 20 minutes. Drain, and pat dry with paper towels. Season the ribs with the 1 teaspoon salt and ½ teaspoon pepper.

❖ Preheat an oven to 325°F (165°C).

❖ In a large nonstick frying pan over medium-high heat, warm the vegetable oil. Using tongs, add the ribs and brown evenly on all sides, about 5 minutes. Transfer the ribs to paper towels to drain briefly, then place them in a large, heavy pot or baking dish.

❖ In the same frying pan over medium-high heat, add the onions and sauté, stirring frequently, until browned, about 5 minutes. Add the carrots and sauté until slightly softened, 2–3 minutes longer. Add the garlic and sauté for 1 minute. Stir in the tomato sauce, barbecue sauce and beef stock, reduce the heat to medium-low and simmer for 1 minute to blend the flavors. Pour the tomato sauce mixture over the short ribs and turn to coat evenly.

❖ Bake the ribs, turning every 45 minutes, until the meat is very tender, about 2½ hours.

❖ Season to taste with salt and pepper. Place on warmed individual plates and serve immediately.

Serves 6

Spaghetti with Meatballs

Odds are, if a diner has a children's menu, spaghetti with meatballs is on it. Grown-ups, too, love the simplicity and goodness of this Italian-American dish. Depending on your mood, make the meatballs as small or large as you like, adjusting the frying time as necessary.

4 tablespoons (2 fl oz/60 ml) olive oil

8 green (spring) onions, including the tender green tops, finely chopped

2 cloves garlic, minced

1 teaspoon dried basil, crumbled

½ teaspoon dried thyme, crumbled

3 oz (90 g) Parmesan cheese, in one piece

2 lb (1 kg) finely ground (minced) lean beef

½ teaspoon salt, plus salt to taste

¼ teaspoon freshly ground pepper, plus pepper to taste

1 egg, beaten

½ cup (2 oz/60 g) fine dried bread crumbs

2 tablespoons finely chopped fresh parsley

1¼ lb (625 g) dried spaghetti

6 cups (48 fl oz/1.5 l) tomato sauce *(recipe on page 14)*

❖ In a small nonstick frying pan over medium-low heat, warm 2 tablespoons of the olive oil. Add the green onions and sauté until almost translucent, 3–4 minutes. Add the garlic and sauté for 1 minute. Stir in ½ teaspoon of the basil and the thyme and cook for 1 minute longer. Set aside to cool.

❖ Grate enough of the Parmesan to measure ¼ cup (1 oz/30 g); set aside. Using a vegetable peeler, shave the remaining Parmesan into thin slices; set aside to use as a garnish.

❖ In a large bowl, combine the beef and the cooked onion-herb mixture. Using your hands, work the seasoning into the meat. Then add the ½ teaspoon salt, the ¼ teaspoon pepper, egg, bread crumbs, reserved grated Parmesan and parsley. Work together until evenly blended. Cover and refrigerate for 30–40 minutes to make the mixture easier to handle.

❖ Form the chilled meat mixture into 1½-inch (4-cm) balls. In a large nonstick frying pan over medium heat, warm the remaining 2 tablespoons oil. Working in batches if necessary, add the meatballs in a single layer; do not allow to touch. Sauté, turning to brown evenly on all sides, about 15 minutes.

❖ Cover the pan, reduce the heat to low and continue to cook until the meatballs are cooked through, about 8 minutes longer. Using a slotted spoon, transfer to paper towels to drain.

❖ Bring a large pot three-fourths full of water to a boil. Salt the water lightly and add the spaghetti. Stir immediately to separate the spaghetti strands and return to a boil. Boil until just tender to the bite, 8–10 minutes, or according to package directions.

❖ While the spaghetti is cooking, in a large, heavy pot or saucepan over medium heat, combine the tomato sauce with the remaining ½ teaspoon basil. Bring to a simmer, add the meatballs, cover and simmer until the meatballs have taken on the flavor of the sauce, 5–7 minutes.

❖ Drain the spaghetti and transfer to a large, warmed platter or individual pasta bowls. Ladle the meatballs and sauce over the noodles and sprinkle with the reserved shaved Parmesan. Serve immediately.

Serves 6

Side Dishes

$\mathcal{T}$ruth be told, many diners need no more than two utensils to prepare most of their side dishes: a can opener and a saucepan. Canned vegetables join potatoes alongside most blue plate specials, only to be consistently ignored by all but the hungriest customers.

But rare diners do exist where vegetables and other side dishes are made from scratch every day: country greens slowly simmered with thick-cut bacon, spinach creamed with a rich white sauce and lightly scented with nutmeg, cabbage and carrots shredded by hand to make coleslaw, potatoes cubed and folded together with a mayonnaise dressing for a classic potato salad. There may be nothing *nouvelle* about such preparations. Few diner vegetables, after all, stand much of a chance of being cooked only until tender-crisp. But, for that very reason, such side dishes are undeniably flavorful.

Also tasty are the wide range of diner quick breads. It will take even the most harried cook no more than a few minutes to mix up a batch of corn bread or biscuits. Hot from the oven and slathered with butter, these breads are guaranteed to make breakfast, lunch or dinner memorable.

Buttermilk Biscuits

Flaky biscuits like these are a grand diner tradition. Using shortening—as in this recipe—or lard produces a flakier biscuit. For a slightly softer crust, lightly brush the hot biscuits with melted butter when they come out of the oven.

2   cups (10 oz/315 g) all-purpose (plain) flour

2½   teaspoons baking powder

½   teaspoon salt

½   teaspoon baking soda (bicarbonate of soda)

½   cup (4 oz/125 g) vegetable shortening, chilled

¾   cup (6 fl oz/180 ml) buttermilk, chilled

❖ In a bowl, stir together the flour, baking powder, salt and baking soda until well mixed. Add the shortening and toss to coat with the flour mixture. Using a pastry blender, 2 knives, or your fingertips, and working quickly, cut or rub in the shortening until the mixture is the consistency of coarse meal.

❖ Make a well in the center of the flour mixture. Pour in the buttermilk all at once, then stir with a fork just until a soft dough forms that pulls away from the sides of the bowl.

❖ Preheat an oven to 450°F (230°C).

❖ Gather the dough into a ball and turn out onto a lightly floured work surface. Knead very gently 5 or 6 times just until the dough holds together. Gently pat or roll out the dough about ½ inch (12 mm) thick.

Using a round biscuit cutter 2 or 2½ inches (5 or 6 cm) in diameter, cut out as many rounds as possible, pressing straight down and lifting the cutter straight up without twisting. Place the dough rounds about 1½ inches (4 cm) apart on an ungreased baking sheet. Very gently knead the scraps together 2 or 3 times and cut as before. Do not reroll any additional scraps.

❖ Bake until evenly browned, 10–12 minutes. Serve hot from the oven.

Makes 12–14 biscuits

SIDE DISHES

Corn Bread

Although corn was a native American crop, early colonists were the first to make bread from the ground meal. Wholesome, savory-sweet corn bread remains a staple in diners nationwide but particularly in the South and Southwest, where corn remains a staple crop. Serve with split pea soup (recipe on page 36) or barbecue-style braised short ribs (page 74).

1 cup (5 oz/155 g) yellow cornmeal
1 cup (5 oz/155 g) all-purpose (plain) flour
1 teaspoon salt
1 tablespoon baking powder
1 cup (8 fl oz/250 ml) milk
2 tablespoons honey
2 eggs, well beaten
⅓ cup (3 oz/90 g) unsalted butter, melted and cooled
½ cup (3 oz/90 g) corn kernels (fresh or thawed frozen)

❖ Preheat an oven to 400°F (200°C). Grease an 8-inch (20-cm) square baking pan with butter.

❖ In a large bowl, mix together the cornmeal, flour, salt and baking powder. In a large measuring cup, whisk together the milk, honey and eggs.

❖ Using a wooden spoon, stir the egg mixture into the cornmeal mixture, mixing well. Stir in the melted butter and then gently mix in the corn kernels. Pour the batter into the prepared pan.

❖ Bake until the center is firm to the touch, 18–20 minutes. Cut into squares and serve hot.

Serves 6

Beer-Battered Onion Rings

*In some parts of the country, fried onion rings are as popular a companion to hamburgers as french fries.
If you don't have an electric deep-fat fryer, choose a good heavy pan, place it safely on a rear burner and
use at least 3 inches (7.5 cm) of oil. To ensure even browning, avoid overcrowding the pan.*

3   large yellow onions
2   cups (16 fl oz/500 ml) milk, chilled
2   cups (16 fl oz/500 ml) ice water

BATTER
1⅓ cups (7 oz/220 g) all-purpose (plain) flour
1   teaspoon salt
1   tablespoon dry mustard
¼   teaspoon freshly ground pepper
2   eggs, at room temperature
2   tablespoons vegetable oil
¾   cup (6 fl oz/180 ml) beer, at room temperature
    Dash of Tabasco or other hot-pepper sauce

    Vegetable oil for deep-frying

❖ Slice the onions crosswise about ½ inch (12 mm) thick and then carefully separate the slices into rings. (You should have about 8 cups/1¾ lb/875 kg.) Place the rings in a wide, shallow dish in as few layers as possible.

❖ In a bowl, whisk together the milk and ice water. Pour evenly over the onions. Cover the dish with plastic wrap and refrigerate for at least 2 hours or as long as overnight. Very carefully turn the rings at least once to soak them evenly.

❖ Meanwhile, make the batter. In a large bowl, whisk together the flour, salt, dry mustard and pepper; set aside. In a bowl, lightly beat the eggs; whisk in the vegetable oil, and then the beer and Tabasco, mixing well.

❖ Make a well in the center of the flour mixture and pour in the egg mixture all at once. Using a whisk and starting in the center of the bowl and working outward, whisk until the mixture is free of lumps. Cover and let stand for at least 2 hours or as long as overnight.

❖ Line 2 baking sheets with a double layer of paper towels. Using tongs, remove the onion rings from the milk mixture, shaking off the excess liquid, and let drain on one of the prepared sheets. Pat the onion rings dry with more paper towels to remove all excess moisture.

❖ In a deep-fat fryer or large, heavy saucepan over medium-high heat, pour in vegetable oil to a depth of at least 3 inches (7.5 cm). Heat until the oil registers 375°F (190°C) on a deep-fat frying thermometer, or until a small cube of bread dropped into the oil browns in about 45 seconds.

❖ Stir the batter. Working in batches and using the tongs, dip the onion rings into the batter, shaking off any excess; quickly but carefully drop them into the hot oil. Fry the onion rings, turning occasionally with the tongs, until a deep golden brown, 4–5 minutes.

❖ Transfer the cooked onion rings to the other paper towel–lined baking sheet and let drain briefly. Serve immediately.

Serves 6

Tricolor Coleslaw

The Dutch cabbage salad, koolsla, *arrived in America soon after the War of Independence.*
Today, many variations of the salad accompany sandwiches or fried chicken in diners, and this
colorful version, tossed with a creamy sweet-and-sour dressing, is one of the best.
Serve it alongside a triple-decker club sandwich (recipe on page 48).

DRESSING
3 tablespoons cider vinegar
1 tablespoon sugar
2 cups (16 fl oz/500 ml) mayonnaise
¼ teaspoon salt
¼ teaspoon freshly ground pepper
3 tablespoons finely chopped fresh
   parsley

SALAD
½ small head red cabbage, shredded
   (about 3 cups/9 oz/280 g)
1 small head green cabbage, shredded
   (about 5 cups/15 oz/470 g)
2 carrots, peeled and shredded
   (about 1 cup/5 oz/155 g)

❖ To make the dressing, in a large serving bowl, stir together the vinegar, sugar, mayonnaise, salt, pepper and parsley until well blended.

❖ Add the shredded red cabbage, shredded green cabbage and shredded carrot to the dressing and, using tongs, toss to coat all the vegetables evenly.

❖ Cover with plastic wrap and chill for at least 2 hours or for up to 8 hours before serving.

Serves 6–8

Potato Salad

*Especially in deli-style diners, potato salad is a staple accompaniment to sandwiches. It has been
a regular feature on the American table since the 19th century. If you can find tiny new potatoes, by all
means use them; otherwise, any red potato 2 inches (5 cm) or less in diameter will work fine.*

1 teaspoon salt
2½ lb (1.25 kg) small red potatoes, unpeeled
3 celery stalks, cut into slices ¼ inch (6 mm) thick
¼ cup (1½ oz/45 g) finely diced red (Spanish) onion

DRESSING
½ cup (4 fl oz/125 ml) sour cream
½ cup (4 fl oz/125 ml) mayonnaise
1 tablespoon mustard seeds
1 green (spring) onion, including the tender green tops, finely chopped
¼ cup finely chopped fresh parsley
1 teaspoon dry mustard
¼ teaspoon salt
⅛ teaspoon freshly ground pepper
1 tablespoon finely chopped fresh parsley

❖ Bring a large saucepan three-fourths full of water to a boil. Add the salt and then the potatoes. Boil until tender but slightly resistant when pierced with a fork, 15–25 minutes depending upon the size. Drain and, when cool enough to handle, cut the unpeeled potatoes into 1-inch (2.5-cm) pieces.

❖ In a bowl, combine the potatoes, celery and red onion and toss briefly to mix. Set aside.

❖ To make the dressing, in a small bowl and using a fork, stir together the sour cream, mayonnaise, mustard seeds, green onion, parsley, dry mustard, salt and pepper, mixing well.

❖ Pour the dressing over the potato mixture. Using a large spoon, mix well, being careful not to break up the potatoes too much.

❖ Transfer the salad to a large serving platter or bowl, if desired. For the best flavor, cover and chill for up to 2 hours before serving. Sprinkle the parsley over the top and serve.

Serves 6

Creamed Spinach

Frozen spinach works beautifully in this simple side dish, as long as you remember to let it thaw, then dry it out well before sautéing. Using a blender ensures a delicately smooth and creamy consistency. Creamed spinach is delicious served alongside fried chicken with a side of fried green tomatoes.

2 tablespoons unsalted butter

4 packages (10 oz/315 g each) frozen chopped spinach, thawed and squeezed dry

1 clove garlic, minced

1 tablespoon all-purpose (plain) flour

1 cup (8 fl oz/250 ml) milk or half-and-half (half cream)

½ teaspoon salt
Pinch of freshly ground pepper
Pinch of ground nutmeg

❖ In a large frying pan with high sides over medium heat, melt the butter. When the foam subsides, add the spinach and sauté, stirring to break it up, just until wilted, 4–5 minutes. Add the garlic and sauté for 1 minute longer.

❖ Sprinkle the flour over the spinach, stir to incorporate and sauté until the spinach is cooked and slightly thickened, about 2 minutes. Add ½ cup (4 fl oz/125 ml) of the milk or half-and-half and cook until the liquid is absorbed, about 1 minute longer.

❖ In a blender, combine the spinach mixture with the remaining ½ cup (4 fl oz/125 ml) milk or half-and-half. Blend until puréed, 1–2 minutes. (Using a rubber spatula, push down 2 or 3 times to purée it evenly.)

❖ Transfer the puréed spinach to a saucepan over medium heat and stir in the salt, pepper and nutmeg. Heat to bubbling, spoon into a warmed serving dish and serve immediately.

Serves 6–8

Collard Greens with Bacon

A time-honored tradition in southern kitchens, collard greens are typically cooked for a long time to temper their tough texture and smooth out their bitter flavor; cooking them a day ahead and then reheating makes them all the better. The greens go perfectly with rich main dishes, such as fried chicken (recipe on page 66).

2 teaspoons olive oil

6 slices thick-cut bacon, chopped

2 large cloves garlic, minced

⅛ teaspoon salt

¼ teaspoon freshly ground black pepper

⅛ teaspoon cayenne pepper

2 tablespoons cider vinegar mixed into 2 cups (16 fl oz/500 ml) water

5 bunches collard greens, about 5 lb (2.5 kg) total weight, stemmed and carefully washed

   Tabasco or other hot-pepper sauce, optional

❖ In a large stockpot over medium heat, warm the olive oil. Add the bacon and fry, stirring constantly, until cooked through but not crisp, 3–4 minutes. Remove the pot from the heat and, using a slotted spoon, transfer the bacon to a dish. Set aside. Pour off all but 2 tablespoons of the drippings from the pot.

❖ Return the stockpot to medium heat. Add the garlic, salt and black and cayenne peppers and sauté for 1 minute. Carefully pour in the vinegar-water mixture, stirring until blended. Return the bacon to the pot and boil for 1–2 minutes.

❖ Reduce the heat to medium-low and add the greens. (Do not worry if the pan is very full; the greens will cook down.) Cover and simmer for 10 minutes, then remove the lid and stir well. Add a few drops of Tabasco, if desired, re-cover and reduce the heat to very low. Simmer, stirring occasionally and adding a little water if needed to keep the greens damp, until the greens are tender, about 1½ hours.

❖ Spoon the greens into a warmed serving dish and serve immediately.

Serves 4

Candied Yams

The dark, orange-fleshed variety of sweet potato commonly known as the yam has been a southern staple since colonial times, and candied yams have enjoyed wide popularity since the late 19th century—especially at Thanksgiving. Try them alongside roast turkey with mashed potatoes and gravy (recipe on page 62).

5   yams or sweet potatoes, unpeeled, about 4 lb (2 kg) total weight

TOPPING
1   cup (7 oz/220 g) firmly packed dark brown sugar
½   cup (4 oz/125 g) unsalted butter, at room temperature
½   cup (2 oz/60 g) finely chopped walnuts
1   teaspoon pumpkin pie spice, or ½ teaspoon ground cinnamon and ¼ teaspoon each ground nutmeg and allspice

❖ Preheat an oven to 425°F (220°C).

❖ Wrap each yam in aluminum foil, pierce all over with a fork and place on a baking sheet. Bake the yams until tender when pierced with a sharp knife, about 1 hour.

❖ Remove the yams from the oven, and reduce the oven temperature to 400°F (200°C). Unwrap the yams immediately and let cool. Using your fingers or a sharp knife, peel the yams and cut crosswise into slices 1 inch (2.5 cm) thick.

❖ To make the topping, in a bowl, combine the brown sugar, butter, walnuts and pumpkin pie spice. Using a fork or your fingertips, mix until coarse and crumbly.

❖ Lightly butter an 8-inch (20-cm) square baking dish. Place half of the yam slices in the prepared dish, arranging them in a single layer. Sprinkle evenly with half of the topping. Layer the remaining yam slices on top and sprinkle with the remaining topping. Place the baking dish on a baking sheet. Bake until the topping melts and is bubbling, 15–20 minutes.

❖ Spoon onto warmed plates and serve immediately.

Serves 6–8

Baked Beans

Dried beans saw early American settlers through many a long, cold winter. Nonperishable, protein-rich, and flavorful, baked beans have been a necessity and a favorite for generations. These beans are even better reheated the following day. Serve with hamburgers or grilled hot dogs.

2½ cups (1 lb/500 g) dried small white (navy) or Great Northern beans
1 yellow onion, coarsely chopped
¼ cup (3 oz/90 g) dark molasses
2 tablespoons firmly packed light brown sugar
1 tablespoon dry mustard
1 tablespoon Worcestershire sauce
½ cup (4 fl oz/125 ml) apple cider
2 tablespoons bourbon whiskey
¼ cup (2 fl oz/60 ml) tomato sauce, homemade *(recipe on page 14)* or purchased
½ teaspoon salt
¼ teaspoon freshly ground pepper
1 cup (8 fl oz/250 ml) water
½ lb (250 g) cooked ham, preferably honey baked, cut into ¼-inch (6-mm) cubes

❖ Pick over the beans, discarding any stones, and rinse with water. Place in a bowl, add water to cover by 2 inches (5 cm) and let soak overnight. Drain.

❖ Bring a large saucepan three-fourths full of water to a boil. Add the drained beans and onion and return to a boil. Reduce the heat to medium-low, cover partially, and simmer until very tender, 1–1½ hours. Drain well and set the beans aside.

❖ Preheat an oven to 350°F (180°C). In a saucepan over medium heat, combine the molasses, brown sugar, mustard, Worcestershire sauce, apple cider, whiskey, tomato sauce, salt, pepper and water. Bring to a simmer, stirring until the sugar dissolves. Continue cooking for 1–2 minutes to blend the flavors.

❖ In a 1½-qt (1.5-l) baking dish, combine the beans and the sauce and mix well. Add a little more water if the mixture looks dry. Stir in the ham. Cover and bake for 35 minutes. Uncover and raise the heat to 400°F (200°C). Continue baking until the liquid is almost gone, 45–60 minutes.

❖ Serve immediately, or let cool, cover and refrigerate overnight. To reheat, bring the chilled beans to room temperature, then place in a 375°F (190°C) oven until heated through, about 25 minutes.

Serves 6

Desserts

Throughout the meal, they beckon you from a high display case behind the counter, backed by a tilted mirror that gives an even better perspective on golden crusts, meringue toppings, and swirls of chocolate frosting. From the moment you take your seat, you can't help but think: What will I have for dessert?

In addition to being irresistible, diner desserts have another characteristic in common. Created in a small, crowded environment in which mealtimes are predictably frenzied, the recipes in this chapter can all be made in advance. Only a few final flourishes—a scoop of ice cream, a spoonful of sauce, a swirl of whipped cream—are necessary before serving.

And what wonderful variety results from such constraints. Healthful apple desserts, their fruit baked whole or sliced and tucked beneath a crisp oat topping. Pies filled with seasonal fruit, lemon curd or coconut custard. Shortcakes overflowing with summer's plump berries. Slow-baked bread or rice puddings. Layer cakes and cheesecakes and brownies. And, of course the banana split—the ultimate soda fountain creation.

Flip through the photographs on the following pages and, in true diner tradition, plan your own menu around a mouth-watering final course.

Spiced Baked Apples

Glance at the dessert display in almost any diner and you're likely to see individual dishes of gleaming baked apples. For a more refined version of this time-honored dessert, peel the top third of the skin and sprinkle with cinnamon.

FILLING
¼ cup (1 oz/30 g) pecan halves
⅓ cup (3 oz/90 g) unsalted butter, chilled, cut into small pieces
⅓ cup (2½ oz/75 g) firmly packed light or dark brown sugar
2 tablespoons coarsely chopped dried apricots
2 tablespoons golden raisins (sultanas)
½ teaspoon ground cinnamon
⅛ teaspoon ground cloves
¼ teaspoon ground allspice
⅛ teaspoon ground nutmeg

6 baking apples, such as Rome Beauty
1 cup (8 fl oz/250 ml) apple juice

❖ To make the filling, preheat an oven to 350°F (180°C). Spread the pecan halves on a baking sheet and bake until lightly toasted, 5–7 minutes. Remove from the oven, let cool and chop coarsely. Set aside. Raise the oven temperature to 400°F (200°C).

❖ In a small bowl, combine the butter and sugar. Using your fingertips or a wooden spoon, mix to a paste-like consistency. Stir in the toasted nuts, apricots, raisins, cinnamon, cloves, allspice and nutmeg. Set aside.

❖ Cut a thin slice off the bottom of each apple so that it will stand upright. Working from the stem ends and using a sharp knife, core the apples without piercing the bottoms.

❖ Using a small spoon, stuff the mixture into the cored apples, dividing it equally. Smooth the tops and cover just the filling with aluminum foil.

❖ Place the apples in a 9-by-13-inch (23-by-33-cm) baking dish. Pour the apple juice into the dish. Bake, basting with the dish juices every 15 minutes, until tender when pierced with a knife, 45–60 minutes.

❖ Transfer the baked apples to a platter or individual serving dishes and serve immediately.

Serves 6

Apple Crisp with Dried Cranberries

Easily prepared in large batches, crumb-topped crisps are standard diner fare. This version includes the native American cranberry, which takes its name from kranbeere, *the name bestowed by Dutch settlers who thought the plant's stamen looked like a crane's beak. Serve warm, with a large scoop of vanilla ice cream.*

TOPPING
1   cup (4 oz/125 g) coarsely chopped pecans
¾   cup (4 oz/125 g) all-purpose (plain) flour
½   teaspoon ground cinnamon
¼   teaspoon ground nutmeg
¼   teaspoon ground allspice
⅛   teaspoon ground cloves
    Pinch of salt
¾   cup (2½ oz/75 g) quick-cooking rolled oats
½   cup (4 oz/125 g) granulated sugar
½   cup (3½ oz/105 g) firmly packed light brown sugar
¾   cup (6 oz/185 g) unsalted butter, chilled, cut into small pieces

FILLING
8   Golden Delicious apples, about 2½ lb (1.25 kg) total weight
3   tablespoons fresh lemon juice
½   cup (2 oz/60 g) dried cranberries

❖ Preheat an oven to 350°F (180°C). Butter a 9-by-12-inch (23-by-30-cm) oval baking dish.

❖ To make the topping, spread the pecans on a baking sheet and bake until lightly toasted, 5–7 minutes. Remove from the oven and let cool.

❖ In a large bowl, stir together the flour, cinnamon, nutmeg, allspice, cloves and salt. Add the toasted pecans, rolled oats, granulated sugar, brown sugar and butter. Using your fingertips, rub the mixture together until it resembles coarse crumbs. Set aside.

❖ To make the filling, peel, halve and core the apples, then cut lengthwise into slices ½ inch (12 mm) thick.

Place in a bowl, immediately add the lemon juice and dried cranberries and toss to coat with the juice. Pour the filling into the prepared dish, leveling the surface. Sprinkle the topping evenly over the fruit, pressing down on it lightly and leaving about ¼ inch (6 mm) space between the topping and the pan sides.

❖ Bake until the topping is golden brown and bubbling, 40–45 minutes, covering the top with aluminum foil if the crust begins to overbrown.

❖ Transfer to a rack and let cool for 15 minutes before serving.

Serves 6

Fresh Peach and Rhubarb Pie

Tangy rhubarb pie has long been a favorite of the Pennsylvania Dutch. Adding fresh summertime peaches to this dessert only makes it better. Peel the peaches only if you care to, as the best end result is a matter of taste. Serve the pie slightly warm, with a big scoop of vanilla ice cream or frozen yogurt.

CRUST

2   cups (10 oz/315 g) all-purpose (plain) flour, plus flour for rolling

½   teaspoon salt

½   cup (4 oz/125 g) unsalted butter, chilled, cut into small pieces

3   tablespoons vegetable shortening, chilled

1   egg yolk

1   tablespoon fresh lemon juice

4–5 tablespoons (2–3 fl oz/60–80 ml) ice water

FILLING

3   rhubarb stalks, cut into ½-inch (12-mm) pieces (about 2 cups/ 8 oz/250 g)

6–7 peaches, peeled or unpeeled, cored and cut into slices ½ inch (12 mm) thick (about 4 cups/ 1½ lb/750 g)

3   tablespoons fresh lemon juice

¾   cup (6 oz/185 g) sugar

¼   teaspoon ground nutmeg

½   teaspoon ground cinnamon

⅓   cup (2 oz/60 g) all-purpose (plain) flour

1   egg beaten with 1 tablespoon water

❖ To make the crust, in a food processor fitted with the metal blade, combine the flour and salt. Process briefly to blend. Add the butter and shortening and process until the mixture resembles coarse meal, 5–10 seconds. With the motor running, gradually add the egg yolk, lemon juice, and just enough of the ice water for the dough to come together and hold a shape when pressed. Remove the dough from the processor, divide into 2 pieces, one slightly larger than the other, and flatten into 2 thick disks. Wrap the disks in plastic wrap and refrigerate for 1–2 hours.

❖ To make the filling, in a large bowl, combine the rhubarb, peaches, lemon juice, sugar, nutmeg, cinnamon and flour and toss until mixed.

❖ On a lightly floured work surface, roll out the larger of the 2 disks into a round about 11 inches (28 cm) in diameter. Gently ease the pastry round into a deep 9-inch (23-cm) pie plate and press into the plate, crimping the edges about ½ inch (12 mm) above the level of the plate rim. Brush the pie crust with the egg-water mixture. Spoon the filling into the dish.

❖ On the lightly floured work surface, roll out the remaining disk into a round about 10 inches (25 cm) in diameter. Using another pie plate as a guide, cut out a 9-inch (23-cm) round from the dough. Cut the round into strips 1 inch (2.5 cm) wide.

❖ Preheat an oven to 425°F (220°C). Brush the edge of the bottom crust with a little more of the egg-water mixture. Lay a row of dough strips ¾ inch (2 cm) apart across the top of the pie. Press the ends firmly to the edge of the crust. Lay the remaining strips in the opposite direction, again pressing them firmly to the edge. Flute the edge decoratively. Brush the pastry edge and strips with the egg-water mixture.

❖ Place the pie on a baking sheet and bake for 10 minutes. Reduce the heat to 350°F (180°C) and continue baking until golden brown and bubbling, 35–45 minutes. (Check the pie during baking and cover the edges with aluminum foil if the crust begins to overbrown.)

❖ Transfer to a rack and let cool for at least 20 minutes before serving. Serve warm or at room temperature.

Makes one 9-inch (23-cm) pie; serves 6–8

Lemon Meringue Pie

A pastry shell filled with lemon curd goes back to European kitchens, but topping it with meringue is an American tradition dating from the 1800s. Take care to measure out all meringue ingredients in advance, because you must make it and spoon it on top of the pie while the filling is still hot.

1   prebaked pie crust *(recipe on page 14)*

FILLING
1   cup (8 oz/250 g) sugar
6   tablespoons (1½ oz/45 g) cornstarch (cornflour)
¼   teaspoon salt
2   cups (16 fl oz/500 ml) water
4   egg yolks, well beaten
3   tablespoons unsalted butter
½   cup (4 fl oz/125 ml) strained fresh lemon juice
    Finely grated zest of 1 large lemon

MERINGUE
5   egg whites
¼   teaspoon cream of tartar
⅛   teaspoon salt
½   cup (4 oz/125 g) sugar

❖ Prepare and bake the pie crust as directed and let cool.

❖ Preheat an oven to 350°F (180°C).

❖ To prepare the filling, in a heavy nonaluminum saucepan, combine the sugar, cornstarch and salt and whisk until smooth. Stir in the water, a few drops at a time at first and then more quickly, never adding more water until the mixture is smooth. Stir in the yolks, whisking well to combine.

❖ Place the saucepan over medium heat and bring to a boil, stirring constantly with a wooden spoon over the bottom and to the edge of the pan. Switch to a whisk occasionally to prevent lumps from forming. When the mixture reaches a boil (7–8 minutes), boil for 1 minute, stirring constantly. Remove the pan from the heat, add the butter and gradually stir in the lemon juice, only a few drops at a time at first, until incorporated and the butter is melted. Stir in the lemon zest. Pour the hot filling into the cooled pie crust, then immediately make the meringue.

❖ To make the meringue, in a large, clean bowl, using an electric mixer set on medium speed, beat the egg whites for a few seconds to break them up. Add the cream of tartar and salt and continue beating until they hold soft peaks, about 2 minutes. Increase the speed to high and add the sugar in a slow, steady stream, stopping occasionally to scrape down the sides of the bowl. Continue beating until stiff peaks form, 2–3 minutes.

❖ Spoon about one-fourth of the meringue on top of the hot filling and spread it to meet the crust. Gently place the remaining meringue in the center of the pie and, using the back of a spoon, shape and spread the meringue into peaks. Bake until the meringue is golden brown and firm to the touch, rotating a few times to promote even coloring, 12–15 minutes. Transfer to a rack and let cool completely.

❖ Serve at room temperature. Or store, uncovered, in the refrigerator for up to 1 day. Bring to room temperature before serving.

Makes one 9-inch (23-cm) pie; serves 6–8

DESSERTS

Coconut Custard Pie

Since the early years of the 20th century, coconut cream pie has been enjoyed in lunchrooms, restaurants and diners across the country. If you like, use the unbaked graham cracker crumb crust used for the strawberry cheesecake (recipe on page 123) in place of the prebaked pie crust.

1 prebaked pie crust *(recipe on page 14)*

1¼ cups (5 oz/140 g) flaked coconut

FILLING
¾ cup (6 oz/185 g) granulated sugar

¼ cup (1 oz/30 g) cornstarch (cornflour)

¼ teaspoon salt

4 egg yolks

3 cups (24 fl oz/750 ml) milk

3 tablespoons unsalted butter

1½ teaspoons vanilla extract (essence)

TOPPING
1 cup (8 fl oz/250 ml) heavy (double) cream

2 tablespoons confectioners' (icing) sugar

½ teaspoon vanilla extract (essence)

❖ Prepare and bake the pie crust as directed and let cool.

❖ Preheat an oven to 375°F (190°C). Spread the coconut in a single layer on a baking sheet with a rim. Bake, stirring several times, until golden brown, 6–8 minutes. Remove from the oven and set aside to cool.

❖ To make the filling, in a heavy nonaluminum saucepan, combine the granulated sugar, cornstarch and salt and whisk to mix well. In a bowl, whisk the egg yolks until blended, then gradually whisk in the milk. Gradually whisk the egg mixture into the sugar mixture, whisking well to dissolve the cornstarch.

❖ Place the saucepan over medium heat and cook for 4–5 minutes, stirring occasionally over the bottom and to the edge of the pan. Switch to a whisk occasionally to prevent lumps from forming. Continue to cook, stirring constantly and whisking occasionally, until the mixture thickens and reaches a boil, 7–9 minutes longer. Boil for 1 minute, stirring constantly, then immediately remove from heat. Stir in the butter,

vanilla and 1 cup (4 oz/120 g) of the toasted coconut. Immediately pour the filling into a bowl, press a piece of waxed paper directly onto the surface and let cool for 15 minutes.

❖ To make the topping, in a large bowl, whisk the cream until semisoft peaks form. Add the confectioners' sugar and vanilla and whisk until soft peaks form. Cover and chill until ready to use.

❖ Pour the filling into the cooled crust and jiggle the dish until the filling is level. Cover and chill until ready to serve. To serve, mound the topping on the pie and sprinkle with the remaining ¼ cup (1 oz/20 g) toasted coconut. Serve immediately.

Makes one 9-inch (23-cm) pie; serves 6–8

Mixed Berry Shortcake

Adding other summer berries to this recipe makes it only more delightful. You can also substitute an equal quantity of peaches, apricots or plums. If you like, replace the whipped cream with a drizzle of heavy cream, a more traditional embellishment.

2 cups (8 oz/250 g) strawberries, hulled and thickly sliced
2 cups (8 oz/250 g) raspberries
2 cups (8 oz/250 g) blackberries
2–3 tablespoons confectioners' (icing) sugar
2 teaspoons Grand Marnier or other orange liqueur

SHORTCAKE
2 cups (10 oz/315 g) all-purpose (plain) flour
1 tablespoon baking powder
½ teaspoon salt
2 tablespoons granulated sugar
6 tablespoons (3 oz/90 g) unsalted butter, chilled, cut into ½-inch (12-mm) pieces
1 cup (8 fl oz/250 ml) heavy (double) cream
1 cup (8 fl oz/250 ml) heavy (double) cream, whipped to soft peaks and chilled

❖ In a large bowl, combine all the berries, the confectioners' sugar and Grand Marnier. Toss to mix. Set aside.

❖ Preheat an oven to 425°F (220°C).

❖ *To make the shortcake in a food processor fitted with the metal blade,* combine the flour, baking powder, salt and granulated sugar. Process briefly to mix. Add the butter and, using on-off pulses, process until the mixture resembles coarse crumbs. With the motor running, slowly add the cream, processing until the mixture forms a soft dough.

❖ *To make the shortcake by hand,* in a large bowl, combine the flour, baking powder, salt and granulated sugar. Using a pastry blender, 2 knives or your fingertips, cut or rub in the butter until the mixture resembles coarse crumbs. Using a fork, gradually mix in the cream until the dough holds together.

❖ Turn out the dough made by either method onto a lightly floured board and knead briefly. Roll out the dough into a 6-by-12-inch (15-by-30-cm) rectangle ½ inch (12 mm) thick. Cut into eight 3-inch (7.5-cm) squares.

❖ Place the squares at least 3 inches (7.5 cm) apart on an ungreased baking sheet. Bake until the tops are light brown, 10–12 minutes.

❖ To assemble, split the shortcakes in half horizontally and place the bottoms, cut side up, on 8 individual dessert plates. Spoon an equal amount of the berries over each shortcake bottom, then spoon an equal amount of the whipped cream over the berries. Place the shortcake top gently over the cream and berries and serve immediately.

Serves 8

Mile-High Chocolate Layer Cake

With a typically American love of exaggeration, any multilayered cake might be dubbed "mile-high."
But watch the expressions when this towering cake is presented, and the name will seem perfectly fitting.
Rich and crumbly on the inside and covered with dense frosting, it's a chocolate lover's delight.

CAKE

2¼   cups (11 oz/360 g) all-purpose (plain) flour
1½   teaspoons baking soda (bicarbonate of soda)
1   teaspoon salt
1¼   teaspoons baking powder
4   oz (125 g) unsweetened chocolate, coarsely chopped
¾   cup (6 oz/185 g) unsalted butter, at room temperature
1¾   cups (14 oz/440 g) sugar
3   eggs
1   teaspoon vanilla extract (essence)
¾   cup (6 fl oz/180 ml) milk

FROSTING

2   cups (16 fl oz/500 ml) heavy (double) cream
15   oz (470 g) semisweet (plain) chocolate, coarsely chopped
⅓   cup (3 oz/90 g) unsalted butter, at room temperature
1½   tablespoons vanilla extract (essence)

❖ Preheat an oven to 350°F (180°C). Butter three 9-inch (23-cm) cake pans.

❖ To make the cake, in a bowl, mix together the flour, baking soda, salt and baking powder. Set aside.

❖ In the top pan of a double boiler or a heatproof bowl set over (not touching) simmering water in a pan, melt the chocolate, stirring until smooth. Remove from the heat and let cool to room temperature.

❖ In a large bowl, using an electric mixer set on medium speed, beat together the butter and sugar until light and fluffy, 3–5 minutes. Add the eggs, one at a time, beating well after each addition. Then add the cooled chocolate and the vanilla and mix until blended. Reduce the speed to low and beat in the flour mixture in three batches, alternating with the milk and beginning and ending with the flour.

❖ Divide the batter evenly among the prepared pans. Tap them on a countertop to rid the batter of any air pockets. Bake until a toothpick inserted into the center of each cake comes out clean, 25–30 minutes. Transfer to racks and let cool in the pans for 15 minutes, then invert the cakes onto the racks to cool completely.

❖ Meanwhile, make the frosting. In a heavy saucepan over high heat, bring the cream to a boil. Remove from the heat and add the chocolate, butter and vanilla, stirring constantly until both the chocolate and butter are melted and the mixture is smooth. Place the pan in the refrigerator and stir every 15 minutes. The frosting will begin to set after about 50 minutes and will be quite thick. Check every 5 minutes near this point for a spreadable consistency. (If the frosting becomes too thick, let stand at room temperature, stirring occasionally, until it softens to a spreadable consistency.)

❖ To frost the cakes, place 1 cake layer, flat side up, on a 12-inch (30-cm) cake plate. Spread the top with one-fourth of the frosting. Place the second cake layer, flat side up, on top of the first, and flatten gently with your hand. Spread the top of the second layer with one-third of the remaining frosting. Place the third layer, flat side up, on top and again flatten gently. Frost the top and sides of the cake quickly, using all of the remaining frosting. Using a flat-edged knife or icing spatula, make quick movements to create swirls on the top and sides of the cake. Let stand for about 1 hour to set the frosting, then serve at room temperature.

Makes one 3-layer, 9-inch (23-cm) cake; serves 10

Fudge Brownies

The difference between a plain brownie and a fudge brownie is that, in the latter, the center stays moist and chewy. These bars are perfect for picnics because, wrapped airtight, they will remain fresh all day. If you like orange flavor with your chocolate, substitute an equal amount of orange liqueur for the vanilla.

¾ cup (6 oz/185 g) unsalted butter

4 oz (125 g) unsweetened chocolate, coarsely chopped

4 eggs

2 cups (1 lb/500 g) granulated sugar

1 teaspoon vanilla extract (essence)

1 cup (5 oz/155 g) all-purpose (plain) flour

½ teaspoon baking powder

½ teaspoon salt

1 cup (5 oz/155 g) chopped almonds

1 tablespoon confectioners' (icing) sugar

❖ Butter a 9-by-13-inch (23-by-33-cm) baking pan. Preheat an oven to 350°F (180°C).

❖ In the top pan of a double boiler or a heatproof bowl set over (not touching) simmering water in a pan, combine the butter and chocolate and stir until melted and smooth. Remove from the heat and let cool.

❖ In a bowl, using an electric mixer set on medium speed, beat together the eggs and granulated sugar until the mixture is thick, pale yellow and holds a trail for 3 or 4 seconds when the beaters are lifted from the batter, 3–4 minutes.

❖ Stir in the vanilla and the cooled butter-chocolate mixture until no streaks remain; do not overmix. Using a rubber spatula, fold in the flour, baking powder and salt until just blended. Fold in the almonds.

❖ Pour the batter into the prepared pan. Bake until a toothpick inserted into the center comes out with some wet crumbs attached, 25–30 minutes.

❖ Transfer to a rack and let cool in the pan. Cut into 2-inch (5-cm) squares. Just before serving, using a fine-mesh sieve or sifter, dust lightly with the confectioners' sugar.

Makes 24 brownies

Banana Split

A quintessential soda fountain concoction, the banana split represents sweet excess at its best.
The two sauces can be made ahead: The fudge sauce can be refrigerated for up to a week and
gently reheated before use; the caramel sauce will keep in the refrigerator for up to 3 days.

½ cup (2½ oz/75 g) slivered
   blanched almonds

FUDGE SAUCE
4   oz (125 g) bittersweet (plain)
    chocolate, coarsely chopped
¼   cup (2 oz/60 g) unsalted butter
¼   cup (2 fl oz/60 ml) heavy
    (double) cream

CARAMEL SAUCE
½   cup (4 fl oz/125 ml) heavy
    (double) cream
½   cup (3½ oz/105 g) firmly packed
    light or dark brown sugar
1   tablespoon unsalted butter

4   ripe bananas
4   scoops vanilla ice cream
4   scoops chocolate ice cream
4   scoops strawberry ice cream
1   cup (8 fl oz/250 ml) heavy
    (double) cream, whipped to soft
    peaks and chilled
4   maraschino cherries, drained

❖ Preheat an oven to 350°F (180°C).
Spread the almonds on a baking
sheet and bake until lightly toasted,
5–7 minutes. Remove from the oven
and let cool.

❖ To make the fudge sauce, in the
top pan of a double boiler or a heatproof bowl set over (not touching)
simmering water in a pan, combine
the chocolate and butter and stir
until melted and smooth. Stir in
the cream just until incorporated.
Remove the pan from the heat,
cover to keep warm and set aside.

❖ To make the caramel sauce, in a
small heavy saucepan over medium-
high heat, stir together the heavy
cream and brown sugar and bring to
a boil. Boil for 2 minutes, stirring
constantly. Add the butter, reduce
the heat to low and simmer until
thick and caramellike, about 2 minutes. Remove from the heat, cover to
keep warm and set aside.

❖ Peel the bananas and cut in half
lengthwise. Lay each banana in an
individual oval dish, cut side up.
Arrange 1 scoop each of vanilla,
chocolate, and strawberry ice cream
on each banana. Drizzle a little
warm fudge sauce over the chocolate
and strawberry ice cream and a little
warm caramel sauce over the top of
the vanilla ice cream. Top with a
mound of the whipped cream, and
then sprinkle with the toasted
almonds. Finally, crown with a
maraschino cherry and serve immediately. Serve the remaining fudge
and caramel sauces on the side.

Serves 4

Chocolate Bread Pudding

Two good reasons explain the enduring popularity of bread pudding in diner kitchens. First, it makes wonderful use of stale bread. Second, it tastes marvelously satisfying. Serve this intensely chocolatey version with a dollop of whipped cream.

6 cups (12 oz/375 g) cubed bread, preferably French or egg bread (¾-inch/2-cm cubes)

4 oz (125 g) unsweetened chocolate, coarsely chopped

3 cups (24 fl oz/750 ml) milk

3 eggs

1¼ cups (10 oz/315 g) granulated sugar

2 teaspoons vanilla extract (essence)

2 tablespoons confectioners' (icing) sugar

❖ Preheat an oven to 350°F (180°C). Butter a 1½-qt (1.5-l) soufflé dish or baking dish.

❖ Spread the bread cubes on a baking sheet. Bake until dry but not browned, 5–7 minutes. Remove from the oven and set aside.

❖ In the top pan of a double boiler or a heatproof bowl set over (not touching) simmering water in a pan, combine the chocolate and milk and stir until the chocolate melts and the mixture is smooth, 5–7 minutes. Remove from the heat and let cool for 10 minutes.

❖ In a bowl, using an electric mixer set on high speed, beat the eggs until blended. Add the granulated sugar and beat until slightly thickened, 1–2 minutes. Reduce the speed to low and gradually beat in the vanilla and the chocolate-milk mixture until incorporated.

❖ Place the bread cubes in the prepared dish. Pour the chocolate custard over the bread and, using a spoon, turn the mixture so that all the bread cubes are evenly soaked with the custard mixture.

❖ Bake for 20 minutes. Then, using a large flat spoon, push down on the bread so the custard rises to the top. Continue baking until the custard is just set, 15–20 minutes longer.

❖ Transfer to a rack and, using a sieve or sifter, lightly dust the top with the confectioners' sugar. Serve warm or at room temperature.

Serves 6

DESSERTS

Rice Pudding with Golden Raisins

Creamy rice pudding is a comforting conclusion to any meal. The delicate texture of medium-grain white rice contributes to its luscious, moist consistency. Raisins are a typical embellishment, but you can add other dried fruits, such as apricots, cherries or cranberries.

5   cups (40 fl oz/1.25 l) half-and-half (half cream)

1   cup (7 oz/220 g) medium-grain white rice

¾   cup (6 oz/185 g) granulated sugar

2   egg yolks

1   teaspoon vanilla extract (essence)

½   teaspoon ground cinnamon

2   tablespoons unsalted butter, at room temperature

¾   cup (4½ oz/140 g) golden raisins (sultanas)

    Cinnamon sugar

    Heavy (double) cream, whipped to soft peaks and chilled (optional)

❖ In a large saucepan over medium-high heat, combine the half-and-half and rice and bring to a boil. Reduce the heat to medium-low and simmer, stirring occasionally at the beginning and constantly the last few minutes to avoid scorching, for about 18 minutes. The rice should be soft, the mixture should be very creamy, and not all of the liquid should be absorbed. Remove from the heat and stir in the granulated sugar, mixing well.

❖ In a small bowl, whisk together the egg yolks, vanilla and cinnamon until blended. Add ½ cup (4 fl oz/125 ml) of the rice mixture, whisking to blend. Return the egg yolk–rice mixture to the saucepan and mix well. Add the butter and raisins and stir until evenly distributed.

❖ Pour the pudding into a 1-qt (1-l) serving bowl and let cool to room temperature. Sprinkle with cinnamon sugar and serve with whipped cream, if desired.

Serves 6

Strawberry Cheesecake

Jewish and Italian immigrants alike brought their own distinctive versions of cheesecake to America. The kind most likely to be found in diners is more typically Jewish, and is now widely known as New York style. If you like, make this particular recipe with a combination of jams and fruit; apricots or plums are especially good.

CRUST

1½ cups (4½ oz/140 g) graham cracker (wholemeal biscuit) crumbs

2 tablespoons granulated sugar

6 tablespoons (3 oz/90 g) unsalted butter, melted

FILLING

3 packages (8 oz/250 g each) cream cheese, at room temperature

1¼ cups (10 oz/315 g) granulated sugar

6 eggs, at room temperature

2 cups (16 fl oz/500 ml) sour cream, at room temperature

⅓ cup (2 oz/60 g) all-purpose (plain) flour, sifted

2 teaspoons vanilla extract (essence)

Finely grated zest and juice of 1 lemon

½ cup (5 oz/155 g) strawberry jam

½ cup (2 oz/60 g) finely chopped, hulled strawberries

12 whole strawberries, hulled

❖ Preheat an oven to 350°F (180°C). Grease a springform pan 9½ inches (24 cm) in diameter and 3 inches (7.5 cm) deep with butter.

❖ To make the crust, in a bowl, combine the crumbs, sugar and melted butter, breaking up any large crumbs and mixing well. Firmly press the mixture evenly over the bottom and about 2 inches (5 cm) up the sides of the prepared pan.

❖ To make the filling, in a large bowl, break the cream cheese into pieces. Using an electric mixer set on medium speed, beat until soft and creamy, about 3 minutes. Add the sugar and beat until the mixture is smooth, 1–2 minutes. Add the eggs, one at a time, beating well after each addition. Reduce the speed to low and beat in the sour cream, flour, vanilla and lemon zest and juice until thoroughly blended.

❖ Remove 1 cup (8 fl oz/250 ml) of the batter and place it in a small mixing bowl. Add the strawberry jam, mixing thoroughly, and then gently mix in the chopped strawberries. Pour this mixture into the rest of the batter and stir just until incorporated. Pour into the prepared pan and jiggle the pan until the batter is level.

❖ Bake for 1 hour. Turn off the heat and allow the cheesecake to rest undisturbed in the oven until set, about 30 minutes longer. Transfer to a rack and let cool. Cover and chill overnight before serving.

❖ Just before serving, run a knife around the pan sides to loosen the cake. Release the pan sides and place the cake on a plate. Arrange the whole berries evenly around the top, marking a slice with each berry.

Makes one 9½-inch (24-cm) cake; serves 12

Glossary

The following glossary defines common ingredients, equipment and cooking procedures used in American diners.

Apple Cider

The drink of the common man in colonial America, cider endures as a national favorite. Sweet apple cider is the unfiltered juice, bottled straight from the apple press. Allowed to ferment to an alcohol level of 3–7 percent, it becomes hard cider. Good-quality cider may be found in apple-growing regions and well-stocked markets.

Baking Powder

Diner quick breads, pancakes and waffles rely for their leavening on this product, used in America since the 1850s. Baking powder consists of three ingredients: baking soda, the source of the carbon-dioxide gas that causes the dough or batter to rise; an acid, such as cream of tartar, calcium acid phosphate or sodium aluminum sulphate, which, when the powder is combined with a liquid, causes the baking soda to release its gas; and a starch such as cornstarch (cornflour) or flour, to keep the powder dry.

Baking Soda

Also known as bicarbonate of soda or sodium bicarbonate, this active component of baking powder is often used on its own to leaven batters that include acidic ingredients

such as buttermilk, yogurt or citrus juices.

Basil

A sweet, spicy herb often used in diners as a seasoning in Italian dishes.

Berries

Juicy and sweet, freshly picked—and, sometimes, frozen—berries are a popular ingredient in diner desserts and breakfast dishes. Four of the most popular berries, used in this book, are:

Blueberries Small, round berries with smooth, blue skins. In season from late spring to summer.

Blackberries Large black to purple-black berries. At their peak of season in summer.

Boysenberries A cross between blackberries, loganberries and raspberries. In season during the late summer.

Strawberries Plump, red, juicy and intensely sweet when ripe. At their peak from spring to midsummer.

Breads

For preparing the specialties in this book, you need only seek out the best mass-produced loaves diner cooks have used

since the 1920s. Try presliced white, sourdough, whole-wheat and rye, as well as egg enriched breads such as challah and brioche.

TO MAKE BREAD CRUMBS
Fresh or dried bread crumbs can add body and texture to meat loaves and stuffings, or can form a crisp coating on fried foods. To make bread crumbs, choose a good-quality white loaf with a firm, coarse-textured crumb.

FOR FRESH BREAD CRUMBS
Slice off the crusts, crumble into a blender or food processor fitted with the metal blade, and process until fine crumbs form.

FOR DRIED BREAD CRUMBS
First make fresh crumbs. Then spread them on a baking sheet and place in an oven set at its lowest temperature until the crumbs are dry, about 1 hour. Store in an airtight container at room temperature. Fine dried bread crumbs are also sold prepackaged in food markets.

Buttermilk

True buttermilk, an American farmhouse favorite, is the tangy, butter-flecked liquid left over when whole milk has been churned to make butter. Most commercial buttermilk sold in food stores, however, is a cultured form of the drink made by adding lactic-acid bacteria to low-fat or nonfat milk. It adds a pleasantly sour taste and thick, creamy texture to muffins, quick breads, pancake and waffle batters.

Butternut Squash

The Narraganset tribe gave Americans the name for squash, from their word *askútasquash,* and tribes all over the northeastern United States introduced both the edible-skinned summer varieties and hard-shelled winter varieties to European settlers. The tan-skinned butternut squash, one of the most popular winter varieties, is large and elongated, with one end almost spherical; it has bright orange, slightly sweet flesh. Also known as pumpkin squash.

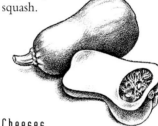

Cheeses

Versatile, flavorful and nourishing, cheese is a staple of the diner kitchen.

Cheddar English settlers brought with them this firm, creamy, whole-milk cheese, which ranges in color from pale yellow-white to deep yellow-orange and in flavor from mild and sweet when fresh to rich and sharply tangy when aged.

Monterey Jack A semisoft white melting cheese, mild in flavor and buttery in texture, this California specialty was developed in the mid-19th century by Monterey farmer David Jacks as his own version of a cheese made by the friars in the Spanish missions.

Parmesan America's grated topping of choice for pasta

dishes, this hard, thick-crusted cow's milk cheese—named for the Italian city of Parma—has a sharp, salty flavor resulting from at least two years of aging. Seek out imported Italian varieties, the best of which are designated Parmigiano-Reggiano® (from the town of Reggio). For the best flavor, buy in block form, to grate fresh as needed.

Swiss Cheese This generic term describes any American type of Swiss Emmenthaler, a firm cheese with a pale yellow color; a mild, slightly sweet, nutlike flavor; and distinctive holes throughout.

Chili, Jalapeño

A popular seasoning of the Southwest, the jalapeño chili has spread nationwide. The small, thick-walled fiery chili is usually sold green, although red ripened specimens may sometimes be found.

Chili Powder

Refers to any of a wide variety of commercial spice blends for seasoning chili con carne and other spicy dishes. Along with ground dried chili peppers, it may also include such seasonings as cumin, oregano, cloves, coriander, pepper and salt. It is best purchased in small quantities, as its flavor will diminish rapidly after opening.

Chili Sauce, Bottled

A popular table condiment in the West, Southwest and South, this commercial bottled blend of hot and mild chili peppers, vinegar, sugar, flavorings and, often, tomato purée also finds its way into the kitchen as a seasoning.

Chocolate

Chocolate has been manufactured in the United States since colonial times. While domestic products will make delicious desserts, you might want to try imported Swiss or other European chocolates for the more complex flavor they contribute.

Semisweet Chocolate This form of chocolate, used for both eating and baking, is usually slightly sweeter than bittersweet chocolate, which may be substituted. Both are also known as plain chocolate.

Unsweetened Chocolate Also known as bitter chocolate, this is pure, unsweetened cocoa liquor, consisting of half cocoa butter and half chocolate solids, pressed into blocks. Although it is extremely bitter tasting on its own, it provides intense chocolate flavor when combined with sugar and butter, milk or cream.

Corned Beef

A specialty of both Jewish and Irish cooking, corned beef is a large cut of beef—usually brisket—that has been cured for about a month in a brine with large crystals (or corns, an old English term) of salt, sugar, spices and preservatives. The result is meat that, when simmered in water, has a moist, tender texture, a mildly spiced flavor and bright purplish red color. Good corned beef may be bought, whole as a brisket and ready to cook, in good-quality butcher shops; delicatessens sell it already cooked, either whole or sliced.

Cornmeal

A Native American staple for more than two thousand years, cornmeal—a granular flour ground from dried kernels of yellow or white corn—was readily adopted as a bread-making staple by the earliest European settlers. Most commercial cornmeal sold in markets lacks the kernel's husk and germ and is available in fine or coarser grinds.

Cornstarch

Also known as cornflour. Ground from the endosperm of the corn kernel—its white heart—this fine powder is used as a flavorless thickening agent for a variety of puddings and pie fillings.

Cream of Tartar

A by-product of wine making, this acidic powder is often added to meringue topping mixtures to stabilize the egg whites and increase their tolerance to heat.

Grilling

Whether done outdoors or inside, cooking on a metal grid—or grill—over the direct heat of a charcoal, wood or gas fire, or an electric coil, is one of the most popular forms of cooking in America. Grilled foods develop a crisply seared exterior that seals in their juices; and the combination of the smoke from the fire and any marinades or bastes that might be used imparts an unmatched savor.

TO BUILD AN OUTDOOR GRILL FIRE
The most reliable heat source is charcoal, whether in the form of compact briquets or lumps of hardwood charcoal from mesquite, hickory or other fragrant woods. Mound the charcoal with fire-starter blocks, or put it in an efficient chimney starter with crumpled newspaper at the bottom, and ignite. The coals will be ready for cooking when they are thinly covered with gray ash or, at night, glow red. Use a metal poker to spread them out in an even bed, then place the grill on top.

Ham, Honey-Baked

Any of a number of commercial varieties of cooked, ready-to-eat American hams that have included honey in the curing process to give the meat a special sweetness. A good-quality sugar-cured ham may be substituted.

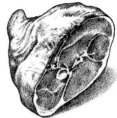

Hot-Pepper Sauce (Tabasco)

A form of bottled hot-chili sauce, made from fresh or dried red chilies, vinegar and salt, used in the kitchens and on the tables of diners in the South and Southwest. Although many commercial brands are available, the best-known is Tabasco, a trademarked product of the McIlhenny company of Avery Island, Louisiana.

Maple Syrup

Native Americans of the northeastern United States first showed European settlers how to derive a rich, sweet syrup by boiling the sap of the sugar maple tree, and maple syrup became a specialty of New England. Seek out maple syrup that is labeled "pure," rather than a blend.

Mustard

Mustard, an Old World spice first brought to America by English settlers, is sold in three basic forms: whole seeds; powdered, often referred to as dry mustard; and prepared. Popular among the prepared types are:

Dijon-Style Mustard Pale, fairly hot and sharp tasting, Dijon mustard is made in Dijon, France, from powdered dark brown mustard seeds (unless marked *blanc*) and white wine or wine vinegar; true Dijon mustard and non-French blends labeled "Dijon-style" are widely available.

Diner-Style Mustard Two varieties of American mustards are likely to be found on the tables of diners: thick, pungent brown mustard reminiscent of German prepared mustards; and a bright yellow, sharp-tasting, more fluid paste seasoned with turmeric, vinegar, white wine and sugar, sometimes called ballpark mustard.

Oats, Quick-Cooking Rolled

More oats are grown in the United States than anywhere else in the world. While most are used as animal feed, tens of millions of bushels find their way to America's tables in the form of breakfast cereals and breads, as well as in toppings for baked desserts. The quick-cooking rolled variety, a popular and widely available form, is made by cleaning and hulling the oats, then flattening them with heated rollers.

Onions

Onions form an indispensable part of the diner pantry. The two most commonly used types are *red (Spanish) onions,* a mild, sweet variety with purplish red skin and red-tinged white flesh; and *yellow onions,* the common white-fleshed, strong-flavored variety with dry, yellowish brown skins.

PREPARING PEARL ONIONS Small but pungent pearl onions about ¾ inch (2 cm) in diameter, also known as pickling onions, are a frequent addition to soups and stews.

1. To peel pearl onions, using a small, sharp knife, trim off the root ends. Cut a shallow X in each trimmed end (to keep the onions whole during cooking). In a pot, combine the pearl onions with plenty of water to cover. Bring to a boil; boil for about 2 minutes, then drain.

2. When cool enough to handle, slip off the skins by squeezing gently with your fingers.

Oregano

Aromatic, pungent and spicy Mediterranean herb used fresh or dried as a seasoning for all types of savory dishes, especially tomato-based dishes. Also known as wild marjoram.

Potato Masher

Although potatoes can be mashed in an electric mixer, nothing beats mashing potatoes the old-fashioned way—by hand. Use a sturdy masher with a flat, stainless-steel perforated grid or bent wire securely attached to a simple handle. Alternatively, mash potatoes with a ricer, a hinged device that forces them through small holes.

Potatoes

Irish immigrants first brought the potato to Massachusetts in the early 18th century, but it took more than 100 years for the vegetable to gain widespread popularity in America. Dozens of different kinds of potatoes may be found today, depending on the region and the time of year. They all may be divided into several broad categories. The potato varieties specified for the recipes in this book are:

Baking Potato Also known as russets or Idahos, these large potatoes have thick brown skins and, when cooked, dry, mealy textures. They are ideal for baking, mashing or frying.

Red Potato Medium-sized potatoes with thin red skins and crisp, waxy-textured white flesh. Good steamed, boiled or roasted.

White Potato Medium-sized potatoes with thin tan skins

and a texture finer than that of baking potatoes but somewhat coarser than that of red potatoes. A good all-purpose choice for cooking.

Relish
In America, the term relish refers to any savory-sweet preserve of vegetables or fruits—flavored with vinegar, salt, sugar and spices—prepared for use as a condiment, especially on hamburgers and hot dogs. The most common types are pickle relishes, sometimes still referred to by the old-fashioned term *piccalilli*. Sweet green pickle relishes tend to have a sweeter flavor than more tangy green pickle relishes.

Shortening, Vegetable
In baked goods, this solid form of vegetable fat is sometimes used in place of or along with butter, to "shorten" the flour—that is, to make it flaky and tender.

Thermometers
Simple cooking thermometers help ensure good results when following a recipe. An *instant-read thermometer,* inserted into the thickest part of a roast near the end of a specified cooking time, will indicate when the meat is done; a *deep-fat frying thermometer,* suspended in the oil while it heats, will show when the desired frying temperature has been reached, as well as act as a guide for adjusting the heat during frying.

Thyme
One of the most popular seasonings, this fragrant, clean-tasting herb, used fresh or dried, complements poultry, meats, seafood or vegetables.

Vinegars
Although the word *vinegar* comes from the French *vin aigre,* or "sour wine," it refers to any alcoholic liquid caused to ferment a second time by certain strains of yeast, turning it highly acidic. Vinegars reflect the qualities of the alcoholic liquid from which they are made. *Red wine vinegar,* for example, has a more robust flavor than vinegar produced from white wine. *Cider vinegar* possesses the crisp tang of apple cider.

Waffle Iron
President Thomas Jefferson reputedly brought to the United States one of the first waffle irons in North America, purchased on a trip to France. Although it was held over a fire by a long handle, it essentially worked in the same way that most electric waffle irons do today, enclosing a batter securely between two patterned metal grids attached by a hinge.

Worcestershire Sauce
A traditional English seasoning or condiment widely popular in America, Worcestershire sauce was developed in the late 19th century when ·a barrel of vinegar and spices, mixed to a customer's specifications, was accidentally left for several years in the basement of the Lea & Perrins chemist's shop in the town of Worcester. The intensely flavorful, savory blend includes molasses, soy sauce, garlic, onion and anchovies, and is popular in marinades or as a table sauce for grilled meat.

Zest
The thin outer layer of a citrus fruit's peel, which contains most of its aromatic oils and provides lively flavor to both sweet and savory dishes.

TO REMOVE CITRUS ZEST
You can remove the zest with a simple tool known as a zester, drawn across the fruit's skin to cut the zest in thin strips *(see below);* with a fine hand-held grater; or in wide strips with a vegetable peeler or a paring knife held almost parallel to the fruit's skin. Zest removed with a zester or vegetable peeler may then be finely chopped.

Acknowledgments

Diane Rossen Worthington extends her thanks to Carla Fitgerald Williams for her recipe testing assistance.

For providing use of their business properties as settings for this book, the publishers, photographer and stylist would like to thank:

Beth and Stephen Simmons of Bubba's Diner, San Anselmo, CA

Lloyd Sugarman, Mike Hampton and Ramiro Saucido of Johnny Rockets, San Francisco, CA

Francisco Padilla of Lori's Diner, San Francisco, CA

Gabriel Mendez and Soi Ha of Mel's Drive-in Restaurant, San Francisco, CA

Hossein Malek of Mo's Restaurant, San Francisco, CA

Howard Ulene, Paula Giorgio, David Spector and Pamela Willson of The Original Mel's, Berkeley, CA

For lending photographic props the photographer and stylist would like to thank:

Another Time Antiques San Francisco, CA

Beaver Bros. Antiques Cookin' San Francisco, CA

Divorson's, San Francisco, CA

J. Goldsmith Antiques and Prop Shop, San Francisco, CA

Naomi's American Dinnerware San Francisco, CA

Vintage Modern, San Francisco, CA

For their valuable editorial support, the publishers would like to thank:

Ken DellaPenta, Liz Marken, Stephani Grant, Marguerite Ozburn, Claire Sanchez and Laurie Wertz.

Photo Credits

Pages 2-3: Cindy Lewis
Page 8: Richard J. S. Gutman

Index

DINER: THE BEST OF AMERICAN CASUAL COOKING